What's For Dinner Mrs. Skinner?

By Kay Skinner
with Peggy Ware

If you desire additional information regarding recipes or about Skinner quality products, please write:

Marketing Department
Skinner Macaroni Company
6848 "F" Street
Omaha, Nebraska 68117

Published by
Keyway Books, Inc.
11 Park Place
New York, N.Y. 10007

Cover photograph by Seymour Mednick;
kitchenware courtesy of Dione Lucas Gourmet Centers, Inc.

CONTENTS

Preface—INTRODUCING
MRS. SKINNER   1
THE LORE OF PASTA   3
Economy Value   5
How Much Should You Buy?   6
How Much To Cook?   6
How To Cook Pasta   7
Leftovers   9
How Should You Eat Pasta?   10
KAY SKINNER'S BUFFET FAVORITES   13
PASTA WITH MEAT   25
PASTA WITH POULTRY   49
MEATLESS PASTA DISHES   58
SAUCES FOR PASTA   70
SNACKS, APPETIZERS AND
SIDE DISHES   77
SALADS   84
GOURMET DISHES   92
QUICK & EASY PASTA DISHES   109
SPECIAL NO-PRECOOKING
PASTA RECIPES   116
PRIZE-WINNING RECIPES   125
FROZEN PASTA   134
CALORIE-CUTTING PASTA DISHES
AND WEIGHT-CONTROL MENUS   142

MONEY-SAVER PASTA DISHES   158
PASTA ALFRESCO   171
PROFITABLE PASTA DINNERS FOR
    CHURCH GROUPS AND CLUBS   176
DECORATING WITH PASTA   189

APPENDIX   195
    A Pasta Lover's Primer   195
    Glossary of Pasta Shapes   196
    How Pasta Is Made   204
    The Nutritive Value of Pasta   207
    Metric Table   210
INDEX   211

INTRODUCING MRS. SKINNER

Kay Skinner is the wife of the Skinner Macaroni Company board chairman, Lloyd E. Skinner. For many years Kay Skinner and other family members have been collecting great macaroni, spaghetti and egg noodle recipes —hundreds of them. Many of these dishes are served regularly in the Skinner household.

Some time ago the Skinner family decided it wanted to share some more of its favorite recipes with the American public. The first edition of WHAT'S FOR DINNER MRS. SKINNER? was the realization of that desire. The book has been received so well that this is its third edition. It is now the world's largest selling all-pasta cookbook.

At the Skinners', as in most American homes, the word "macaroni" carries a dual meaning. It refers specifically to the familiar hollow tubes of fairly large diameter. It also is the generic term for all the myriad shapes and sizes of boiled wheat dough—from macaroni to spaghetti to noodles, from shells to twirls to alphabets, from manicotti to lasagne to vermicelli.

Because this has led to so much confusion of terms, many people, including the Skinners, have adopted the traditional Italian word *pasta* (from *pasta alimentare*, meaning nourishing paste) to represent the whole range and scope of macaroni products.

1

A food with a rich history, nutritious, adaptable, inexpensive and decorative, pasta occupies a position of eminent practicality among modern convenience foods.

—PEGGY WARE

THE LORE OF PASTA

Legend credits the great Venetian, Marco Polo, with the introduction of pasta to Europe. He is supposed to have brought it back from the Orient with him in the early fourteenth century. It is highly probable that pasta in one form or another did originate in China, but many centuries before Marco Polo. Now historians (Italian ones, understandably enough) have turned up evidence that pasta was being eaten in Europe long before Marco Polo was even born—the first mention of it having been discovered in an illuminated manuscript that was copied in 1200. Sorry about the whole thing, Marco.

In truth, the origins of pasta are veiled in the mists of time, told and retold in fable and folklore.

In the days of King Frederick of Swabia, there lived a man named Cicho who, with the onset of years, said to himself, "I must find some means of giving happiness to all mankind before I die . . . a delicious dish, perhaps, concocted to suit everyman's taste." Repairing to his kitchen, Cichò experimented with a great variety of simple, nutritious foodstuffs. After many failures, success rewarded his efforts. But before he could present his discovery to the people, a neighbor woman, who had all this time been spying on Cicho, prepared the dish and

3

presented it to the king. Highly pleased, the monarch named it *"macaroni,"* from the word *macarus*, the divine dish.

When poor Cicho protested that the invention was his, he was told, "An angel revealed the recipe to the king's cook. Macaroni is a blessing from heaven." Cicho shrugged, bowed his head, shuffled home to his kitchen and closed the door. He was never seen again.

On a more cheerful note, the tale is told of a wealthy nobleman of Palermo, many centuries ago, who was noted for his love of fine food. The pride of his life was the chef who ran his kitchen, a man of marvelous invention. One day this culinary genius devised a new food from wheat paste in the form of tubes. He served it, covered with a rich sauce and sprinkled with grated Parmesan cheese, in a large china bowl.

The first mouthful brought forth from the illustrious epicure a shout of *"Cari!"* which in idiomatic English means, "The darlings!"

His second mouthful produced, *"Ma Cari!"*—"What darlings!"

As the flavor and delicate texture of the dish grew upon him, his enthusiasm rose to even greater heights and he cried out, *"Ma Caroni!"*—"What dearest darlings!"

Whatever its origin, the word macaroni had come to have a special meaning in England in the 1770's, a meaning that accompanied macaroni when it was brought to America at the time of the American Revolution and made immortal in song:

> "Yankee Doodle went to town
> Riding on a pony.
> Stuck a feather in his hat
> And called it 'Macaroni'."

In England the term "macaroni" was a synonym for perfection and elegance. It was common practice for the English to use the slang phrase "That's macaroni" to describe anything exceptionally good. So, when the English soldier wrote the song about Yankee Doodle sticking a feather in his hat, he signified that the feather was an object of elegance.

The meaning has never been lost and has even migrated back to sunny Italy—if it ever left, for that's where it may well have originated.

If you hire a horse-drawn vehicle in Naples today, when you pay your fare and give the driver his tip, he will descend from his perch, smile and say, "For macaroni." Likely as not he's referring to his horse. The custom of nicknaming cab horses macaroni began during Italian festival days when the stallions were decked out in flowers and wreaths, to which a crowning touch was a long pheasant feather fastened to the bridle. This was superb, the height of elegance, "macaroni!"

Ah, macaroni, a food of many delights, a word of many variant meanings—*too* many. This book will stay with "pasta," a word of broad, but explicit, meaning.

ECONOMY VALUE

Pasta is so low priced in today's market place it can be served in a great variety of ways to really s-t-r-e-t-c-h your food dollar. Because of its high nutritive value and good protein content, it is an excellent supplement to meats, which are substantially higher in price. Meats account for a third of the average family's food expenditures. Serving pasta enables you to buy smaller quantities of expensive meats. For example, served by itself, you should allow 4 ounces per person of ground beef, or 1½ pounds to serve six people. But if you make a meat sauce to serve over spaghetti, you only need 1 pound of ground beef for six servings. This cuts your meat cost by one third. Pasta as a side dish supplements the protein content of any meal; it satisfies you.

Prices of pasta products are the same week after week and are not affected by seasonal supplies which change the price structure of many foods, both fresh and processed. Although there is a special chapter in this book on money-saving pasta dishes, as you glance through these pages you will find many other recipes to help stretch your food budget.

Without denying its fine flavor, it's safe to say that the low cost of pasta helped make it a national dish in Italy. Serving pasta every day was the answer to raising a large family on a limited income. Perhaps in our present economy of rising costs, we should adopt the same custom and get the best possible value for our grocery dollar.

HOW MUCH SHOULD YOU BUY?

Since pasta products keep so well, it is practical to buy several packages at a time, or at least to keep a reserve supply of the types your family likes best. Pasta is one of your best food bargains today. The convenience and short cooking time of macaroni, egg noodles and spaghetti make them valuable for hurry-up meals and un-expected guests. Several package sizes are sold to meet family needs—usually in logical increments of 8-ounce, 12-ounce, 16-ounce, 24-ounce, 32-ounce, 48-ounce and larger. Refer to the back of the book for an illustrated glossary of the most popular pasta shapes.

HOW MUCH TO COOK?

This really depends on the appetites of your family members, but a general rule is to allow 4 ounces of un-cooked pasta per person for a main dish. Some families would consider a somewhat smaller or larger serving per person more practical. Macaroni and spaghetti approxi-mately double in volume after cooking, while egg noodles remain about the same in volume.

Considering that 16 ounces will usually provide 4 servings, the following table will be helpful in determining the amount to cook when one type of pasta is substituted for another, and in deciding how much to cook for a desired number of servings.

16 ounces product	*Uncooked*	*Cooked*
Spaghetti (unbroken)	——	8⅔ cups
Elbow macaroni	4 cups	8 cups
Shells (small)	4¾ cups	8 cups
Egg noodles	8 cups	8 cups
Frozen egg noodles	——	6 cups

Whenever practical in this book, the cup measurement is given as well as the weight. Since the number of pieces of a given pasta shape that will fill a cup varies slightly from time to time, cup measurements are approximate. Measurements of cooked cups also can vary since pasta to a degree continues to absorb water the longer it is cooked. A few small pieces, more or less, will not be critical in any recipe, however. For recipes listing frozen egg noodles, buy the package size nearest the specific amount of noodles you need, as frozen pasta should *not* be thawed before cooking.

HOW TO COOK PASTA

Pasta is easy to cook with perfect results every time if you follow these basic directions. For 8 ounces of spaghetti, macaroni or egg noodles:

1. Heat 3 quarts of water to a *rapid* rolling boil.
2. Add 1 tablespoon salt. (You can add 1 to 1½ teaspoons salad oil or olive oil to keep the water from boiling over and to help keep the pasta separated.)
3. *Gradually* add 2 cups (8 ounces) macaroni, or 8 ounces (about 4 cups) egg noodles, or 8 ounces spaghetti. With spaghetti, grasp a handful and place one end of the strands in the water. As the strands soften gently push them into the water, until all of them are submerged. Be sure the water *continues* to boil.

The rapid and continuous boiling helps to keep the pasta moving about so that it will cook quickly and evenly. The pasta should be added slowly while the water continues to boil so there is no chance that the strands or pieces stick together. If boiling is not maintained during the cooking period, the pasta may also settle to the bottom of the cooking vessel, where the pieces may clump together; the weight of the pasta can cause shape distortion, or pieces on the outside of the mass may overcook before those at the center are done.

4. Cook, *uncovered*, stirring occasionally and gently, until tender. Stirring also helps to keep the pasta evenly distributed and moving in the boiling water so that all of it will be cooked at the same time. Always read the package directions and do not overcook.

5. Test for doneness by tasting a piece. Pasta properly cooked should be *tender* yet *firm*—as the Italians say, *al dente,* "to the tooth." Cooking time will vary with the size and thickness of macaroni product used. Very thin pasta products may cook in 2 minutes, while some thicker shapes may require 15 minutes; average is 8 to 10 minutes. Cooking time is critical to properly prepared pasta; be guided by the time indicated on the package. Reduce the cooking time by approximately one-third if the pasta will be used in a casserole and will be cooked further.

6. The moment the pasta is done, immediately drain it in a colander. Serve as quickly as possible (or mix with other ingredients in the recipe); freshly cooked, pasta is at its most delicious. Do *not* rinse unless the pasta is to be used in a cold salad. Then rinse with cold water and drain again. The finished salad is improved if you chill it in a refrigerator about an hour. In addition to bringing it down to the proper temperature, it permits the flavors of the ingredients to blend.

When you are cooking manicotti, rigatoni or lasagne, they must be allowed to cool briefly so that you can handle them to continue preparing the dish.

Special instructions for cooking larger quantities are to be found in the chapter Profitable Pasta Dinners for Church Groups and Clubs, but here's a rule of thumb: For each 16 ounces of pasta use 4 to 6 quarts water and 2 tablespoons salt.

Frozen egg noodles are cooked similarly to dry pasta, but require less water. Bring to rapid boil 12 cups water with 2 tablespoons salt. Add a 16 oz. package, unthawed. Stir until separated. After water returns to boil, cook 15 minutes or until noodles reach desired tenderness. For soups or stews, simply cook noodles same length of time in broth. For oven dishes, reduce cooking time to 10 minutes instead of 15.

LEFTOVERS

As we have said, freshly cooked macaroni, spaghetti and egg noodles are the very best, but there may be some left over, or you may decide to make an extra casserole for the freezer. Lasagne is an excellent example of a dish that freezes well. Pasta freezes beautifully, but from a space viewpoint it may be more practical just to make extra sauce and freeze it in containers according to your recipe or family size. Then you can cook the pasta fresh for each dish and enjoy it at the peak of flavor and texture. In general, low temperatures, such as provided by a double boiler, should be used to reheat cooked pasta without sauce. Just add a tablespoon or two of water and a little butter and heat gently.

Here are a few suggestions for using leftover pasta products in various forms without sauce:

- *To add to soups.* Refrigerate the leftover pasta until ready for use. Then add during last 5 minutes of cooking time to vegetable, tomato, chicken or pea soup, or to consommé or bouillon. Spaghetti may be cut into small lengths, if desired. (Soup can go in the carried lunch by pouring, while still piping hot, into a wide-mouth vacuum bottle, rinsed with hot water.)

- *To make a salad.* Mix together the pasta, small amounts of leftover meats, vegetables. Mix with mayonnaise or salad dressing. Season to taste. Chill and serve on crisp salad greens. (This can go in a carried lunch too. The chilled salad can be spooned into a wide-mouth vacuum bottle that has been rinsed with cold water, or it can be packed in a small plastic container or wrapped in foil.)

- *To add to eggs.* Prepare scrambled eggs or omelet as usual, adding about ½ cup leftover cooked macaroni product for each egg used.

- *To combine with vegetables.* Add macaroni during the last 5 minutes of cooking time to vegetables such as whole-kernel corn, stewed tomatoes, green beans, lima beans, chopped broccoli or spinach.

- *To freeze for future use.* Freeze individual portions or single-meal amounts in plastic freezer containers of appropriate size. To serve, thaw, turn into a casserole. Bake, uncovered, in 375° oven, 20 to 25 minutes, or until piping hot. (Or heat in top of double boiler over hot water.)

- *To pack in carried lunch.* Refrigerate until ready to pack lunch. Reheat individual portion in top of double boiler over hot water. Spoon into wide-mouth vacuum bottle of appropriate size that has been rinsed with hot water. (If necessary, the mixture may be thinned a bit while heating, with milk, tomato juice, bouillon, or whatever liquid was used in the original casserole. This thinned-out mixture may be heated to boiling in a saucepan.)

HOW SHOULD YOU EAT PASTA?

"With gusto!" is the answer to that one. But how do you eat spaghetti? That's a question that does get asked, and the doubt still remains "What is the *proper* way to eat spaghetti?"

Ask an Italian. Surely the native of the country that has enjoyed spaghetti longer than any other will give you a quick and definite answer. Or better, ask for a demonstration. With a gentle but sure grip on the fork, holding it almost upright in the manner of holding a pencil, he sends its tines speeding into the very center of the platter of spaghetti and starts twirling immediately. In the wink of an eye a generous mouthful of the slender pasta strands is wrapped around the fork. The next thing you know the fork is lifted, then it's empty and on its way back to the plate. It's one continuous motion, deft and graceful from start to finish.

The use of a large spoon is probably an American invention. After all, this country has not had the centuries of practice that Italy has had. The desire to handle spaghetti efficiently and gracefully appears to have inspired the use of a second tool. In the double-instrument method the spoon is held in the left hand and the fork is held in the right hand in an overhand manner. The fork is sent through the spaghetti, with its tines resting in the bowl of the spoon while it is being twirled, to gather a supply of spaghetti. Fork and spoon begin the journey to the mouth together but part company just short of the lips. That's one technique. In truth, you make your own rules.

Of course there is another way to eat spaghetti. The cautious diner cuts it up with knife and fork, then scoops it onto the fork to carry it to the mouth. While this is quite practical and causes no serious social repercussions, it doesn't seem very sporting.

Then, of course, there's the child's favorite method. With his fingers he catches hold of one strand of spaghetti, pops it in his mouth and quickly—or slowly, depending on his particular nature—"slurps" it musically all the way to the other end. His face is a picture of bliss as all five of his senses come into play in the sheer enjoyment of it all. It's a deprived child indeed who hasn't been allowed at least a brief interlude with this method before being taught a more acceptable technique.

Take your choice, depending on who you are, where you are and with whom. But don't let self-consciousness about the proper method deter you from eating spaghetti. It's an easy-going dish, meant to be enjoyed.

KAY SKINNER'S BUFFET FAVORITES

Buffets are the preferred mode of entertainment in the Skinner home—where no meal is complete without pasta. Here, in this chapter, are some of Kay Skinner's buffet favorites.

Buffets put extra demands on food. Dishes must hold well, both in flavor and appearance, throughout the serving period. Pasta dishes meet this requirement and have the added advantage of advance preparation—freeing the hostess to be with her guests at party time.

Before trying any new buffet recipe on company, however, it's a good idea to stage a dress rehearsal for your family. Most of the recipes in this chapter are for more servings than the usual family requires, but you can halve them easily enough—or double or triple them for really big parties.

SPAGHETTI AL PESTO

1 pound spaghetti
2 cups firmly packed
    Italian parsley leaves

2 tablespoons fresh basil
    leaves, or 1 teaspoon
    dried

3 garlic cloves
¾ cup olive oil
3 tablespoons butter
½ cup freshly grated
    Romano cheese
½ cup freshly grated
    Parmesan cheese
1½ teaspoons salt
¼ teaspoon pepper

Cook spaghetti as directed on package. Drain. Meanwhile, combine remaining ingredients in electric blender. Blend at high speed until mixture looks almost like a paste, but with some specks of parsley still visible. Toss with spaghetti until spaghetti is completely coated. Serves 8.

SPAGHETTI PAISANO FOR COMPANY

1½ pounds spaghetti
3 pounds Italian sweet
    sausage, cut in 1-inch
    pieces
1½ pounds ground beef
3 medium green peppers,
    thinly sliced
3 8-ounce cans tomato
    sauce
3 6-ounce cans tomato
    paste
3 cups water
1 tablespoon salt
¾ teaspoon basil
Dash of pepper

Brown sausage pieces in Dutch oven, drain on absorbent paper. Lightly brown the beef and green peppers in sausage drippings. Discard drippings. Add sausage, tomato sauce, tomato paste, water, salt, basil and pepper to beef. Cover and simmer 45 minutes, stirring occasionally. Meanwhile, cook spaghetti according to package directions. Drain. Serve with meat sauce. Serves 12.

AS YOU LIKE IT SPAGHETTI AND MEAT BALLS

1 pound spaghetti
2 pounds ground beef
¾ cup chopped onion
¼ cup chopped parsley
3 teaspoons salt
½ teaspoon pepper
2 tablespoons olive oil
3 garlic cloves
2 28-ounce cans plum
    tomatoes

2 6-ounce cans tomato paste

1 teaspoon orégano

1 teaspoon basil

Freshly grated Parmesan cheese

Lightly mix together beef, ¼ cup of the onion, the parsley, 1½ teaspoons of the salt and ¼ teaspoon of the pepper. Shape into 24 meat balls. In Dutch oven or heavy saucepan, brown meat balls in oil. Discard drippings. Add remaining onion and the garlic. Sauté 2 or 3 minutes. Mix in tomatoes, tomato paste, remaining salt and pepper, orégano and basil. Simmer uncovered 30 minutes. Simmer covered 50 minutes longer. Discard garlic.

Meanwhile, cook spaghetti as directed on package. Drain. Serve with the meat balls and sauce. Top with freshly grated Parmesan cheese. Serves 8.

VARIATIONS:

1. Add liquid from a 6-ounce can of sliced broiled mushrooms to the tomato mixture. Add mushrooms the last 10 minutes of cooking time.
2. Add ½ cup sliced pimiento-stuffed olives the last 10 minutes of cooking time.
3. Use only 1½ pounds ground beef and mix with ½ pound ground pork.
4. Sauté 2 medium green peppers, thinly sliced, with onion and garlic.
5. Add ½ to 1 pound sautéed and drained Italian hot or sweet sausages before simmering.

EGG NOODLES AND KÖTTBULLAR

1½ pounds (12 cups) medium egg noodles
⅓ cup minced onion
Butter (about ½ cup)
3 eggs, slightly beaten
6 cups milk
3 cups soft bread crumbs
2 tablespoons salt

Freshly ground pepper
3 pounds ground beef round
¾ pound ground veal
¾ pound ground pork
Flour (about ¾ cup)
⅛ teaspoon nutmeg
3 cups light cream

In a large skillet sauté onion in 3 tablespoons butter until lightly browned; remove with slotted spoon to mixing bowl. Add eggs, 3 cups of the milk, the bread crumbs, 1 tablespoon of the salt, and pepper to taste, to onion; let stand 5 to 8 minutes. Add meats and mix well (divide ingredients in half for ease of handling, if desired); mixture will be soft. Shape into 1½ inch balls and roll in flour. Chill. If necessary roll in flour again. In same skillet, sauté meat balls slowly in additional butter as needed until done. Remove with slotted spoon and keep hot. Quickly stir 6 tablespoons flour into skillet and brown. Gradually stir in remaining 3 cups milk and 1 tablespoon salt, the nutmeg and cream. Cook, stirring, until sauce boils 1 minute.

Meanwhile, cook noodles as directed on package. Serve noodles topped with meat balls and sauce. Serves 12.

LASAGNE A LA MURIEL

8 ounces lasagne	1 1½-ounce envelope
1 pound ground beef	spaghetti sauce mix
2 teaspoons seasoned salt	½ pound mozzarella cheese,
2 garlic cloves, crushed	sliced
¼ teaspoon pepper	½ pound ricotta cheese
2 20-ounce cans tomatoes	½ cup grated Parmesan
1 8-ounce can tomato sauce	cheese

Brown meat in Dutch oven or heavy skillet. Add seasoned salt, garlic and pepper. Cook slowly, uncovered, 10 minutes. Stir in tomatoes, tomato sauce and spaghetti sauce mix. Cover and simmer 30 minutes. Meanwhile, cook lasagne as directed on package. Drain and rinse. Into a baking dish (12x8x2 inches) pour one-third of meat sauce; cover with strips of lasagne, then with slices of mozzarella and spoonfuls of ricotta. Repeat layers, ending with meat sauce. Top with Parmesan cheese. Bake in 350° oven for 20 minutes. Serves 6 to 8.

BAKED STUFFED RIGATONI

8 ounces rigatoni (about 60)
2 tablespoons olive oil
¾ cup chopped onion
1 garlic clove, minced
2 pounds ground beef or pork sausage meat (or · try half and half)
2 eggs, beaten

½ cup dry bread crumbs
3 tablespoons chopped parsley
Salt and pepper
6 cups Basic Tomato Sauce, 1½ times recipe (p. 71)
Grated Parmesan cheese

Cook rigatoni as directed on package. Drain. Cool. Spread out on tray. Heat oil in large skillet; add onion and garlic and cook over medium heat until golden. Add beef and cook, stirring constantly, just until lightly browned. (If using sausage meat, omit oil and place sausage in skillet. Break up into small pieces. Cook, stirring constantly, until lightly browned. Pour off excess fat from skillet; add onion and garlic and cook until golden.) Remove meat mixture from heat and cool slightly. Blend in eggs, bread crumbs and parsley. Season to taste with salt and pepper. Stuff rigatoni with meat mixture.

Arrange stuffed rigatoni in shallow 3-quart casserole. Pour basic tomato sauce over rigatoni. Bake uncovered in 350° oven for 30 minutes, spooning sauce over top occasionally. Serve with Parmesan cheese. Serves 8 to 10.

PARTY MACARONI CHILI

8 ounces (2 cups) elbow macaroni
2 pounds ground beef round
3 tablespoons olive oil
1 28-ounce can tomatoes

1 quart tomato juice
2 cups chopped onions
3 garlic cloves, minced
4 teaspoons salt
2 tablespoons chili powder

½ teaspoon ground cumin
½ teaspoon orégano
½ teaspoon Tabasco
1 bay leaf

1 15-ounce can red kidney beans, drained
1 cup sweet mixed pickles, chopped

In a Dutch oven brown beef in oil, stirring frequently. Add tomatoes, tomato juice, onions, garlic, salt and remaining seasonings. Simmer, covered, 1 hour; stir in kidney beans and pickles. Cook 30 minutes longer. Remove bay leaf. Meanwhile, cook macaroni as directed on package. Drain. Combine with chili. Serve in bowls. Serves 10.

ALL AMERICAN MACARONI CASSEROLE

1 pound (4 cups) elbow macaroni
3 pounds ground beef
2 large onions, chopped
2 medium green peppers, diced
2 6-ounce cans tomato paste
2 15-ounce cans tomato sauce

1 tablespoon salt
1½ teaspoons orégano
¼ teaspoon Tabasco
⅛ teaspoon crushed red pepper
1 pound creamed cottage cheese
2 cups shredded Cheddar cheese

Cook meat in a large kettle, stirring frequently, until browned. Drain off drippings. Add onions and green peppers; cook 1 minute. Stir in tomato paste, tomato sauce and seasonings. Cover and simmer 45 minutes, stirring occasionally.

Meanwhile, cook macaroni as directed on package. Drain. Layer half of macaroni and meat sauce in a 5-quart casserole, or use two 2½-quart casseroles. Spoon cottage cheese on top and sprinkle with 1 cup of the Cheddar cheese. Repeat layers of remaining macaroni, meat sauce and then Cheddar. Bake in 375° oven 15 minutes; cover loosely with foil and bake 20 minutes longer. Serves 12.

FAMILY FAVORITE SPAGHETTI WITH CLAM SAUCE

1 pound spaghetti
4 garlic cloves, crushed
½ cup olive oil
4 7½-ounce cans chopped clams, undrained
1½ cups chopped parsley
½ teaspoon salt
Pepper

Cook spaghetti as directed on package. Drain. Meanwhile, in large saucepan cook garlic in oil until golden; add remaining ingredients. Heat slowly and pour over spaghetti in serving dish. Serves 8.

NOODLE EGGPLANT CASSEROLE

1 pound (8 cups) egg noodles
6 8-ounce cans tomato sauce with mushrooms
1½ cups water
½ cup butter
2 garlic cloves, minced
2½ teaspoons salt
¼ teaspoon pepper
½ teaspoon orégano
2 medium eggplants, cubed
8 ounces mozzarella cheese, sliced

In large saucepan combine tomato sauce, water, butter, garlic, salt, pepper and orégano; bring to a boil. Add eggplant cubes; cover and simmer 30 minutes, or until tender, stirring occasionally.

Meanwhile, cook noodles as directed on package. Drain. Mix noodles with eggplant and sauce; turn into two 2½-quart casseroles. Top with cheese. Cover and bake in 375° oven 30 minutes to heat through. Serves 12.

BUFFET NOODLE CHICKEN CASSEROLE

1½ pounds (12 cups) fine egg noodles
6 chicken breasts, halved
Seasoned salt (about 2 tablespoons)
⅓ cup butter

⅓ cup flour
6 cups milk
4 cups shredded Cheddar
    cheese

¼ teaspoon pepper
½ teaspoon chervil
½ teaspoon thyme

Place chicken pieces in shallow roasting pan; sprinkle with seasoned salt. Bake in 350° oven 45 minutes or until tender.

Meanwhile, cook noodles as directed on package. Drain. Melt butter in saucepan; blend in flour. Gradually add milk; cook, stirring constantly until sauce boils 1 minute. Add cheese, 1 tablespoon seasoned salt, the pepper, chervil and thyme. Heat and stir until cheese melts. Combine noodles and two thirds of the sauce in two 3-quart baking dishes. Top with chicken; pour remaining sauce over all. Bake in 350° oven 20 to 30 minutes. Serves 12.

GUEST CHICKEN CACCIATORE

1½ pounds spaghetti
3 broiler-fryer chickens
    (2½ to 3 pounds each)
    cut in serving pieces
    Flour
½ cup olive oil
3 cups thinly sliced carrots
1½ cups diced celery

6 large tomatoes, peeled
    and chopped
¾ cup chopped parsley
3 tablespoons basil
1 tablespoon salt
1½ teaspoons rosemary
¾ teaspoon pepper
3 cups dry white wine

Dredge chicken with flour. In Dutch oven brown chicken in oil; add carrots and celery; sauté 5 minutes. Add tomatoes, parsley, basil, salt, rosemary, pepper and wine. Cover and simmer 45 minutes, or until chicken is tender. Cook uncovered 5 minutes to thicken sauce. Meanwhile, cook spaghetti as directed on package. Drain. Serve chicken and sauce over spaghetti. Serves 12.

NOODLES AMANDINE

1 pound (8 cups) fine egg noodles	¼ cup butter
1 cup blanched almonds	2 tablespoons poppy seeds

Cook noodles as directed on package. Drain. Meanwhile, chop the almonds coarsely and sauté in the butter until lightly brown. Mix almonds, butter in which they were sautéed and poppy seeds with the noodles. Place in top of a double boiler over low heat, or in a chafing dish, and allow to stand for 30 minutes before serving. Serves 10 to 12.

VERMICELLI ALFREDO

12 ounces vermicelli	½ cup heavy cream, at room temperature
½ pound sweet butter, softened	Freshly ground black pepper
2 cups grated Parmesan cheese	

Cook vermicelli as directed on package. Drain. Place butter in hot casserole; add vermicelli and toss gently. Add cheese and toss again. Pour in cream; toss. Sprinkle with freshly ground black pepper, if desired. Keep warm over *very* low heat. Serves 6 to 8.

SEASHELL PARTY SALAD

4 cups shell macaroni	1 tablespoon Worcestershire
½ cup Italian salad dressing	⅔ cup mayonnaise
2 green onions, thinly sliced	2 tablespoons vinegar
½ cup chopped green pepper	1 teaspoon salad mustard
2 cups diced celery	1 teaspoon salt
2 cups cubed cooked ham	1 teaspoon Tabasco
1 cup cubed Cheddar cheese	1 cup ripe olives, chopped

Cook macaroni as directed on package; drain. Marinate cooked macaroni in Italian dressing; drain. Add vegetables, ham and cheese. In a separate bowl combine remaining ingredients. Toss with macaroni mixture. Serve with crisp salad greens, if desired. Serves 10 to 12.

BELGIUM MACARONI SALAD

1 pound (4 cups) elbow macaroni
2 10-ounce packages frozen Brussels sprouts, cooked, drained, cooled and halved
24 cherry tomatoes, halved
½ cup lemon juice
½ cup salad oil
1½ teaspoons garlic salt
1 teaspoon orégano
¼ to ½ teaspoon pepper
1 pound Swiss cheese, slivered
1½ cups chopped celery
½ cup slivered ripe olives
½ cup coarsely chopped pecans
2 teaspoons salt
1 cup mayonnaise

Combine Brussels sprouts, tomatoes, lemon juice, oil, garlic salt, orégano and pepper; marinate 30 minutes, stirring occasionally.

Meanwhile, cook macaroni as directed on package. Drain. Cool. Add macaroni, cheese, celery, olives, pecans and salt to sprout mixture. Toss lightly; chill. Just before serving, stir in mayonnaise. Garnish with additional cherry tomatoes, if desired. Serves 12.

ZINGY MACARONI SALAD

1 pound (4 cups) elbow macaroni
2 tablespoons chopped green onion
1 cup sliced radishes
1 cup chopped green pepper
1 cup sliced celery
1 cup mayonnaise
3 tablespoons spicy brown mustard
1 tablespoon prepared horseradish
2 teaspoons salt
⅛ teaspoon white pepper

Cook macaroni as directed on package. Drain. Cool. In a large bowl combine macaroni, green onion, radishes, green pepper and celery. Blend together mayonnaise, mustard, horseradish, salt and pepper; toss with macaroni mixture. Chill. Garnish with radish roses, if desired. Serves 12.

COLOSSUS ALMONDINE

*Cheese Sauce:

3 tablespoons butter or margarine	Dash nutmeg
3 tablespoons flour	¼ teaspoon Tabasco sauce
¼ teaspoon onion salt	1¾ cups milk
	½ cup grated Swiss cheese

Melt butter in saucepan; blend in flour, salt, nutmeg and Tabasco. Stir in milk. Cook, stirring constantly, until mixture thickens and comes to a boil. Add cheese; stir until melted. Remove from heat.

Shells and Filling:

6 ounces Colossus Shells (about 18 shells)	1 teaspoon salt
	¼ teaspoon Tabasco sauce
2 10-ounce packages frozen chopped spinach (thawed and well drained)	*½ cup cheese sauce
	2 tablespoons chopped anchovies
2 tablespoons butter or margarine	½ cup toasted slivered almonds
2 tablespoons chopped green onion	½ cup milk

Cook shells as directed on package. Drain. Arrange shells in a greased baking dish. Heat butter in large skillet; add onion and cook until tender, but not brown. Add spinach, salt and Tabasco; cook over low heat 3 to 5 minutes. Add ½ cup cheese sauce, anchovies and almonds and mix well. Stuff shells with spinach mixture. Stir ½ cup milk into remaining cheese sauce and pour over Colossus Shells. Sprinkle with additional grated Swiss cheese and toasted slivered almonds. Bake in 350° oven for 15 minutes or until cheese is bubbly. Serves 6.

CALIFORNIA MACARONI BUFFET SALAD

1½ pounds (6 cups) elbow macaroni

3 8-ounce packages cream cheese, softened

3 medium grapefruit, sectioned

3 medium red apples, unpared and diced

3 ripe avocados, peeled and diced

1½ cups cranberry-orange relish

¾ cup mayonnaise

⅓ cup lemon juice

3 cups black grapes, halved and seeded

1½ cups pecan halves

Cook macaroni as directed on package. Drain. Meanwhile, beat cream cheese until smooth; beat in cranberry relish, mayonnaise and lemon juice until well blended. In large bowl toss together macaroni, cream cheese dressing, fruits and nuts. Chill for 30 minutes before serving. Serves 12.

PASTA WITH MEAT

This chapter concentrates on recipes that utilize meat, although you will find many other meat recipes throughout the book.

With its particular affinity for sauces and gravies, pasta's distinguishing texture and flavor make it perfect for a broad range of casserole and skillet cookery.

OLD-FASHIONED POT ROAST

1 pound (8 cups) wide egg noodles	1¼ teaspoons salt
4 pounds eye of round or beef rump roast	2 beef bouillon cubes
2 tablespoons salad oil	¼ teaspoon pepper
¼ pound mushrooms, sliced	2 bay leaves
2 medium onions, sliced	⅓ cup tomato paste
1 large carrot, halved	1 cup and 3 tablespoons water
1 celery rib, halved	2 tablespoons flour
2 garlic cloves, minced	2 tablespoons chopped parsley (optional)

In a Dutch oven brown meat on all sides in oil. Remove meat and drain off fat. Combine vegetables, garlic, salt, bouillon cubes, pepper, bay leaves, tomato paste and 1 cup water in pan; heat to boiling. Return roast. Cover and simmer 4 hours. Discard carrot, celery and bay leaves. Remove meat to platter; keep warm. Blend flour and 3 tablespoons water; stir into cooking liquid. Cook and stir until gravy boils 1 minute. Stir in parsley.

Meanwhile, cook noodles as directed on package. Drain. Toss with small amount of gravy. Serve with pot roast and remaining gravy. Serves 8.

RIPPLETS AND SAUERBRATEN

12 ounces (6 cups) ripplet egg noodles	2 large bay leaves, crushed
4 to 4½ pounds beef pot roast, tied	1½ teaspoons salt
1 medium onion, sliced	½ teaspoon monosodium glutamate
2 garlic cloves, pressed	3 to 4 tablespoons dark brown sugar
5 whole allspice	1¼ cups water
3 whole cloves	1 cup dry red wine
2 cardamom pods, crushed	¾ cup tarragon vinegar
¼ teaspoon peppercorns	1 tablespoon salad oil
¼ teaspoon mustard seeds	2½ tablespoons flour

Place beef in a large bowl; add onion, garlic, spices, bay leaves, salt, monosodium glutamate, sugar, 1 cup water, the wine and vinegar. Cover and marinate overnight.

Remove beef from marinade; reserve marinade with all ingredients. Pat meat dry to prevent spattering. In Dutch oven, brown meat slowly in oil. Drain off any excess fat. Add reserved marinade to beef. Cover tightly and simmer gently about 3½ hours, or until fork tender. Remove beef from gravy; keep hot. There should be about 2½ cups gravy; bring to a boil. Blend flour into ¼ cup water. Quickly stir into boiling gravy; cook, stirring constantly, until gravy boils 1 minute. Strain.

Meanwhile, cook ripplets as directed on package. Drain. Surround sauerbraten with ripplets; drizzle ½ cup gravy over ripplets. Serve with remaining gravy. Serves 6 to 8.

EGG NOODLES WITH HUNGARIAN GOULASH

8 ounces (4 cups) wide
    egg noodles
1½ pounds onions, thinly
    sliced
3 tablespoons butter
1½ pounds cubed beef

1 tablespoon paprika
2 teaspoons salt
¼ teaspoon pepper
3 cups water
2 tablespoons poppy seeds
    (optional)

In a large saucepan sauté onions in butter about 5 minutes; add beef cubes, paprika, salt, pepper and water. Simmer covered 1½ to 2 hours, or until meat is tender, stirring occasionally. Meanwhile, cook noodles as directed on package. Drain. Toss with poppy seeds. Serve goulash over noodles. Serves 4.

BEEF CURRY WITH NOODLES

8 ounces (4 cups) medium
    egg noodles
1 pound beef round, cut in
    ¾-inch cubes
Flour
Salt and pepper
¼ cup salad oil
2 cups sliced onions

1 small garlic clove, finely
    chopped
1½ teaspoons curry powder
1 cup beef bouillon
2 tablespoons butter
2 tablespoons flour
1 cup milk

Dredge beef with flour, salt and pepper. Cook in oil until browned on all sides. Add onions and garlic and cook until onions are browned. Add 1 teaspoon of the curry powder and the bouillon. Cover and cook over low heat 1¼ hours, or until beef is tender, stirring occasionally. In small saucepan, melt butter and blend in 2 tablespoons flour and remaining curry powder. Gradually add milk and cook over low heat, stirring constantly, until thickened. Gradually stir into beef mixture and mix well.

Meanwhile, cook noodles as directed on package. Drain. Pour beef curry over noodles. Serve with mango chutney, flaked coconut, pineapple chunks and chopped green pepper. Serves 4.

MACARONI AND SHORT RIBS

2 cups elbow macaroni	1 teaspoon orégano
2 pounds or more beef short ribs	2 carrots, cut in ½-inch slices
1 tablespoon salad oil	1 turnip, peeled and diced
1½ cups water	1 medium onion, coarsely cut
⅓ cup catsup	cut
1 teaspoon salt	Paprika
⅛ teaspoon pepper	

Cut short ribs into serving pieces. Brown in oil over medium heat until crusty and brown. Add water, catsup, salt, pepper and orégano. Cover and simmer slowly—1 hour. Add vegetables and continue simmering 1 hour longer. Cook macaroni as directed on package. Drain. Arrange macaroni on large platter, heaping high in center. Place short ribs at either end. Spoon sauce over them. Sprinkle with paprika. Serves 4.

MOSTACCIOLI BEEF PIE

12 ounces mostaccioli	1 cup fine bread crumbs
1¼ pounds round steak, cut in ½-inch cubes, or ground beef	1 28-ounce can tomatoes
	Salt and pepper
4 tablespoons butter	1 cup chopped onions

Cook mostaccioli as directed on package. Drain. Brown meat in 2 tablespoons of the butter. Cover, and cook on low heat until tender, about 30 minutes. Put half of bread crumbs into the bottom of a 3-quart casserole. Then in layers, add meat, tomatoes lifted from juice, and mostaccioli. Sprinkle each layer with salt and pepper.

Sauté onions in remaining 2 tablespoons butter until yellow. Add remaining bread crumbs and toss until crumbs have absorbed butter, then arrange this mixture to form top layer of the pie. Dot with additional butter, if desired. Combine juice from canned tomatoes with enough water to make 1 cup. Pour mixture over pie. Bake in 350° oven for 30 minutes. Serves 6.

MACARONI MEAT LOAF

8 ounces (2 cups) elbow macaroni
¼ cup butter
¼ cup flour
1¾ teaspoons salt
¼ teaspoon pepper
1¼ cups milk

1 cup heavy cream
3 cups grated Cheddar cheese
1 egg, slightly beaten
1½ cups prepared bread stuffing
1½ pounds ground beef

Cook macaroni as directed on package. Drain. Meanwhile, melt butter in saucepan; blend in flour, ¾ teaspoon salt and ⅛ teaspoon pepper. Gradually add milk and cream. Cook over low heat, stirring constantly, until thickened. Add cheese; stir until melted. Mix macaroni with cheese sauce. Mix together egg, prepared stuffing, beef, remaining salt and pepper. Spread on bottom of baking pan (13x9x2 inches). Cover with macaroni mixture. Bake in 400° oven 35 minutes. Serves 6.

EASY LASAGNE

8 ounces lasagne (about 10 pieces)
2 pounds ground beef chuck
1 medium onion, chopped
¼ cup chopped green pepper
2 15-ounce cans spaghetti sauce

1 3-ounce can chopped broiled mushrooms, undrained
Salt and pepper
½ pound mozzarella cheese, thinly sliced
Grated Parmesan cheese

Brown meat in large skillet; drain off excess fat. Stir in onion, green pepper, spaghetti sauce, mushrooms and salt and pepper to taste. Simmer covered 30 minutes or longer. Meanwhile, cook lasagne as directed on package. Drain. Layer sauce, lasagne and mozzarella in shallow rectangular baking dish. Sprinkle grated cheese on top. Bake in 350° oven about 35 minutes, or until piping hot. Serves 6.

BAKED STUFFED MANICOTTI

- 8 ounces manicotti (14 pieces)
- 4½ cups ricotta cheese (about 2½ pounds)
- 1 cup grated Parmesan cheese
- ¼ pound prosciutto, finely chopped (about ⅔ cup)
- ⅓ cup chopped Italian parsley
- 2 egg yolks, beaten
- 2 tablespoons milk
- ½ teaspoon salt
- ⅛ teaspoon white pepper
- Cream sauce (see next page)

To prepare filling, mix together ricotta cheese, ¾ cup Parmesan, prosciutto, parsley, egg yolks, milk, salt and pepper; chill. Prepare cream cauce. Pour small amount of sauce into 2 baking pans (13x9x2 inches). Cook manicotti as directed on package. Drain of ¾ of the water; add enough cold water to stop cooking and cool the manicotti for handling.

Lift manicotti one at a time from water. Using a tea-spoon or pastry tube, stuff with cheese mixture and place in baking pan. Repeat, using remaining manicotti and cheese filling. Arrange filled manicotti side by side in a single layer; the pans should be filled. Pour remaining sauce on top. Cover with foil and bake in 350° oven 30 minutes. Uncover and sprinkle additional Parmesan cheese over all. Broil lightly under broiler. Serves 8.

NOTE: Manicotti must be removed from water and

stuffed one at a time in order to keep them moist for easy handling and filling.

Cream Sauce: In medium saucepan, sauté ½ cup chopped onion in ⅓ cup butter until almost tender. Stir in ⅓ cup flour, 1½ teaspoons salt and ¼ teaspoon white pepper. Gradually add 1½ cups chicken broth, 2 cups light cream, and 1 cup milk. Cook, stirring constantly until sauce boils; remove from heat. Blend in 3 tablespoons tomato paste. Makes 5 cups.

MANICOTTI MAGNIFICO

8 ounces manicotti (14 pieces)	1¾ teaspoons basil
1 pound Italian sweet sausage links	1½ teaspoons salt
	1 teaspoon sugar
1¼ cups water	½ teaspoon pepper
1 pound ground beef	2 pounds ricotta or cottage cheese
1 medium onion, chopped	
2 1-pound cans tomato purée	8 ounces mozzarella cheese, diced
1 6-ounce can tomato paste	2 tablespoons chopped parsley
	Grated Parmesan cheese

Cook manicotti as directed on package. In covered Dutch oven cook sausage links in ¼ cup water 5 minutes. Uncover; brown sausage links well. Drain on absorbent paper, discard drippings.

Brown ground beef and onion well. Stir in tomato purée, tomato paste, 1 teaspoon basil, 1 teaspoon salt, the sugar, pepper and 1 cup water; simmer covered, 45 minutes. Cut sausage into bite-size pieces; add to mixture; cook 15 minutes more.

In large bowl combine ricotta and mozzarella cheeses, parsley, remaining basil, ½ teaspoon salt; stuff in cooked manicotti. Spoon half of meat sauce into baking pan

(13x9 inches). Arrange half of stuffed manicotti over sauce in one layer. Spoon remaining sauce except ¾ cup over them, top with remaining manicotti in one layer. Spoon reserved meat sauce over top. Sprinkle with Parmesan cheese. Bake in 375° oven 30 minutes or until hot. Serves 8.

SAM'S HEARTY BEEF CASSEROLE

8 ounces shell macaroni
1 pound ground beef
1 1-pound can tomato
    sauce
8 ounces cottage cheese
1 8-ounce package cream
    cheese, softened

½ cup sour cream
⅓ cup chopped green
    onions
1 tablespoon chopped
    green pepper

Cook macaroni as directed on package. Drain. Meanwhile, brown beef in skillet and add tomato sauce. Remove from heat.

Combine cheeses, sour cream, green onions and green pepper. Spread half of the shells in 2-quart casserole. Cover with cheese mixture. Add remaining shells and pour beef-tomato mixture over all. Bake in 350° oven 40 minutes, or until bubbly. Serves 6 to 8.

NOTE: This recipe is a favorite for church suppers.

MEAT BALLS IN CREAM SAUCE

8 ounces (2 cups) ready
    cut spaghetti
2 cups cornflakes
1 pound ground beef or
    veal
1½ ounces salt pork, ground
1½ tablespoons chopped
    onion

1¼ teaspoons salt
⅛ teaspoon pepper
½ cup milk or meat stock
1 teaspoon lemon juice
1 tablespoon shortening or
    drippings
2 cups medium white sauce

Crush cornflakes slightly; combine with beef, salt pork, onion, salt, pepper, milk and lemon juice. Mix well. Shape into balls. Brown meat balls in heated shortening; pour off any excess fat. Arrange meat balls in baking dish; add the white sauce. Bake in 350° oven about 1 hour. Cook spaghetti as directed on package. Drain. Arrange spaghetti on heated platter; cover with meat balls and sauce. Serves 6.

VERMICELLI WITH HERB MEAT SAUCE

12 ounces twisted vermicelli
1 pound ground beef
1 tablespoon shortening
1 1-pound can tomatoes
1 8-ounce can tomato sauce
¼ teaspoon sugar

¼ teaspoon orégano
1 teaspoon seasoned salt
¼ teaspoon basil
¼ teaspoon garlic powder (optional)

In a large skillet, crumble and lightly brown ground beef in hot shortening. Reduce temperature to simmer. Stir in tomatoes with juice, tomato sauce and all seasonings. Cover and simmer 20 to 25 minutes. While sauce is simmering, cook vermicelli according to package directions. Drain. Serve with meat sauce. Makes 4 to 6 servings.

NOTE: The sauce is delicious with all pasta!

SPAGHETTI WITH MEAT SAUCE

1 pound Italian style spaghetti
2 medium onions, chopped
1 garlic clove, minced
¼ cup olive oil
1 pound ground beef chuck
1 10½-ounce can tomato purée
2 cups stewed or canned tomatoes

¾ teaspoon sugar
½ cup dry red wine
½ cup grated Parmesan cheese
1 teaspoon salt
Freshly ground pepper
2 tablespoons chopped parsley

Sauté onions and garlic in olive oil until lightly browned. Add beef and cook, stirring constantly, until meat loses its red color. Add tomato purée, tomatoes, sugar, wine, Parmesan, salt, and pepper to taste. Simmer over very low heat 2 hours, adding more wine if necessary. The sauce should be thick. Cook spaghetti as directed on package. Drain. Serve meat sauce over spaghetti and sprinkle with parsley. Serves 6 to 8. (This dish illustrated in color section.)

MACARONI WITH CHILI BEEF SAUCE

12 ounces (3 cups) elbow macaroni
½ pound beef round, diced
½ pound ground beef round
3 tablespoons butter
1 cup chopped onions
2 garlic cloves, minced
1 28-ounce can tomatoes
1 cup water
2 teaspoons salt
1 tablespoon chili powder
1 teaspoon ground cumin
¼ teaspoon cracked bay leaf
¼ teaspoon orégano
¼ teaspoon pepper

In a heavy saucepan brown diced and ground beef in butter. Add onions, garlic, tomatoes, water, salt and seasonings; mix well. Cover and simmer 1 hour and 15 minutes. Uncover and cook 15 minutes longer. Cook macaroni as directed on package. Combine with meat mixture. Serves 6.

SPAGHETTI WITH SWEDISH MEAT BALLS

8 ounces thin spaghetti
1 cup dry bread crumbs
1 tablespoon instant minced onion
½ cup milk
1 egg
2 teaspoons salt
½ teaspoon nutmeg
Dash black pepper (optional)
1 pound ground beef chuck
¾ cup butter, melted
½ cup flour
1 tablespoon tomato paste
¼ teaspoon crumbled dillweed
2 cups water
1 cup sour cream
¼ cup chopped parsley
¼ teaspoon garlic powder

Soak bread crumbs and instant onion in milk. Stir in egg, salt, nutmeg and pepper. Add meat and mix well. Shape into balls, using 1 rounded teaspoon of the mixture for each ball. Fry meat balls in ¼ cup butter until browned on all sides. Remove and keep warm. Measure drippings and add more butter if needed to make ¼ cup. Stir in flour smoothly. Add tomato paste and dill. Gradually add water, stirring constantly, and cook until thickened. Remove from heat and cool slightly. Add sour cream, a tablespoonful at a time, stirring constantly. Return meat balls to sauce. Heat, but do not boil, to serving temperature.

Meanwhile, cook spaghetti as directed on package. Drain. Combine remaining melted butter with parsley and garlic powder. Pour over spaghetti and toss lightly. Arrange on serving platter with meat balls in sauce. Serves 4 to 6.

CHEF'S CASSEROLE

8 ounces (4 cups) medium egg noodles
¼ cup butter
1½ pounds ground beef
1 large onion, chopped
Salt and pepper
1 14-ounce can mushrooms, drained
1 10½-ounce can tomato purée
¼ pound Cheddar cheese, cubed

Cook noodles as directed on package. Drain. Meanwhile, brown beef and onion in butter. Season to taste with salt and pepper. Add drained mushrooms and tomato purée; stir and bring to a boil. Combine with noodles and cheese in 3-quart casserole. Bake in 350° oven about 40 minutes. Serves 6 to 8.

CHILI MOSTACCIOLI

4 cups mostaccioli
1½ pounds ground beef
1½ teaspoons salt
Freshly ground pepper
½ garlic clove, minced
¼ cup chopped onion

6 tablespoons melted
   butter
1 10½-ounce can
   condensed chili-beef
   soup

¼ cup water
¼ pound mushrooms, sliced
¾ cup grated Romano
   cheese

Season meat with salt and pepper. Shape into 6 patties.
Sauté garlic and onion in 4 tablespoons butter until onion
is soft, but not brown. Remove onion and garlic and
brown patties on both sides in the same pan, adding more
butter if necessary. Remove patties. Add soup, water,
garlic and onions to pan and blend thoroughly. Place
patties in mixture and simmer, covered, until they are
done to your taste. Meanwhile, sauté mushrooms in 2
tablespoons butter 5 minutes. Add to sauce.

Cook mostaccioli as directed on package. Drain. Place
on heated platter. Arrange patties like wheel spokes on
top and pour sauce over all. Sprinkle cheese on top.
Serves 6.

BARBECUED MEAT BALLS AND SPAGHETTI

8 ounces spaghetti
1 pound ground beef
2 teaspoons salt
¼ teaspoon pepper
3 tablespoons butter
1 10½-ounce can condensed
   tomato soup

¼ cup sweet pickle relish
2 tablespoons instant
   minced onion
2 tablespoons vinegar
2 tablespoons catsup
1 tablespoon brown sugar

Mix beef thoroughly with 1 teaspoon salt and the pepper.
Form into 1-inch balls. Brown in butter in hot skillet.
Combine soup, pickle relish, onion, vinegar, catsup, sugar
and remaining salt. Add to meat balls, bring to a boil,
reduce heat and simmer, uncovered, for 25 minutes.
Meanwhile, cook spaghetti as directed on package. Drain
and arrange on heated platter. Pour meat balls and sauce
around spaghetti. Serves 4 to 6.

MOSTACCIOLI WITH RICH TOMATO BEEF SAUCE

4 cups mostaccioli	1 teaspoon orégano
½ cup finely chopped onion	Dash of basil
¼ cup diced celery	Dash of thyme
1 4-ounce can mushroom pieces, drained	½ bay leaf
½ garlic clove, finely chopped	1½ teaspoons salt
2 tablespoons salad oil	Dash of pepper
1¼ pounds ground beef chuck	1 20-ounce can tomatoes
	1 6-ounce can tomato paste
	1 cup beef stock

Sauté onion, celery, mushrooms and garlic in oil in heavy saucepan. Add beef and continue cooking until meat begins to brown. Add all other ingredients except mostaccioli. Bring to boil, stirring frequently. Reduce heat and simmer slowly about 1 hour. Meanwhile, cook mostaccioli as directed on package. Drain. Place on heated platter and pour sauce over. Serve with grated Parmesan cheese. Serves 4 to 6.

NOTE: This sauce is delicious with all pasta.

LASAGNETTES

8 ounces (4 cups) wide egg noodles	1 1-pound can tomatoes
2 tablespoons salad oil	Salt and pepper
¼ cup chopped onion	¼ pound mozzarella cheese, sliced
1 pound ground beef round	2 tablespoons grated Parmesan cheese
1 8-ounce can tomato sauce	

Heat oil; add onion and cook until lightly browned. Add beef and cook until browned, stirring occasionally. Add tomato sauce and undrained tomatoes, and season. Cover and cook over low heat 1 hour, stirring occasionally.

Meanwhile, cook noodles as directed on package. Drain. Arrange layers of noodles, beef mixture and cheeses in 6 buttered individual casseroles. Bake in 350° oven 45 minutes. Serves 6.

SWEET AND SOUR MEAT BALLS

4 ounces (2 cups) wide egg noodles
1 pound ground beef
¼ pound ground pork
1 teaspoon salt
Dash of pepper
2 teaspoons minced onion
1 teaspoon Worcestershire
½ cup bread crumbs
1 egg

2 tablespoons milk
2 tablespoons shortening
2 tablespoons light corn syrup
1 teaspoon salt
⅓ cup brown sugar
2 tablespoons cornstarch
⅓ cup cider vinegar
2 teaspoons soy sauce
2 cups water

Mix beef, pork, salt, pepper, onion, Worcestershire, bread crumbs, egg and milk. Shape into small balls. Melt shortening in large heavy skillet. Add meat balls and brown evenly on all sides. Meanwhile, combine corn syrup, salt, sugar, cornstarch, vinegar, soy sauce and water. Cook, stirring constantly, until thickened. Add browned meat balls, bring to a boil, cover, and reduce heat. Simmer 35 to 40 minutes. Cook noodles as directed on package. Drain. Place on hot serving platter and pour meat balls and sauce over. Serves 4 to 6.

CURRIED PORK WITH SPAGHETTI

8 ounces spaghetti
1½ pounds pork shoulder, cut in 2x½-inch strips
2 tablespoons butter
½ cup sliced onion
¼ cup chopped green pepper
1 tablespoon curry powder
1 teaspoon salt

⅛ teaspoon pepper
½ cup and 2 tablespoons water
1⅔ cups (large can) evaporated milk
1 medium apple, cored, pared and shredded
1 tablespoon flour

Brown pork in butter; drain off any excess fat. Add onion and green pepper. Stir in curry powder, salt, pepper and ½ cup water. Bring to a boil. Cover and simmer 45 minutes. Add evaporated milk and apple; cook uncovered 15 minutes longer, or until pork is tender. Blend flour with 2 tablespoons water. Stir into curry; boil 1 minute, stirring, until sauce thickens.

Meanwhile, cook spaghetti as directed on package. Drain. Arrange on hot platter. Pour curry sauce over. Serves 6 to 8.

ORIENTAL PORK NOODLE DINNER

8 ounces (4 cups) egg noodles
½ cup soy sauce
½ cup sugar
½ teaspoon garlic powder
2 tablespoons catsup
½ teaspoon monosodium glutamate
¼ teaspoon salt
1½ pounds lean pork shoulder, cut in ½-inch-thick slices
¼ cup butter, melted
3 tablespoons toasted sesame seeds

Combine soy sauce, sugar, garlic powder, catsup, monosodium glutamate and salt; mix thoroughly. Pour over pork in shallow dish and allow to marinate at least 3 hours.

Drain pork and broil 10 minutes on each side. Cut meat into bite-size pieces. Reserve pan drippings. Meanwhile, cook noodles as directed on package. Drain. Toss with melted butter and sprinkle with sesame seeds. Top with pork and pan drippings. Serves 4.

PORK CHOPS WITH APPLE-SPICE NOODLES

8 ounces (4 cups) wide egg noodles
6 loin pork chops, cut ½-inch thick
Salt and pepper
3½ cups applesauce
½ cup seedless raisins
1 teaspoon salt

1 teaspoon cinnamon	¼ teaspoon ground cloves
½ teaspoon nutmeg	

Cook noodles as directed on package. Drain. Season chops with salt and pepper. Brown in heavy skillet; remove and keep warm. Combine applesauce, raisins, salt and spices in same skillet. Simmer gently 10 minutes to develop flavor, stirring occasionally. Add to noodles, mixing well. Pour into buttered 3-quart casserole. Arrange pork chops on top and cover casserole. Bake in 325° oven 1 hour or until chops are tender. Serves 6.

·HAWAIIAN PORK CHOPS AND MACARONI

2 cups small shell macaroni	½ pound mushrooms, sliced
1 garlic clove, cut	6 slices pineapple
6 pork chops, cut ½-inch thick	Curry Onion Sauce (below)
Salt and pepper	

Cook shells as directed on package. Drain. Spread evenly in a buttered large shallow baking dish. Meantime, rub a skillet with the cut garlic clove. Brown chops well on both sides at medium heat. Season to taste. Remove chops from pan. Add mushrooms and sauté in fat from chops, adding a little butter if necessary, for 5 minutes. Sprinkle over macaroni in baking dish. Arrange chops on top and put a slice of pineapple on each. Pour curry sauce over and bake in 325° oven 1¼ hours, or until chops are tender. Serves 6.

CURRY ONION SAUCE

¼ cup butter	2 teaspoons salt
½ cup minced onion	1 tablespoon curry powder
¼ cup flour	4 cups milk

In skillet in which chops and mushrooms were cooked, melt butter and sauté onion until transparent but not brown. Blend in flour, salt, and curry powder. Gradually add milk, stirring constantly, and cook until thickened and smooth. Makes 4½ cups.

BARBECUED RIBS WITH SPAGHETTI

8 ounces thin spaghetti	¼ cup light brown sugar
4 pounds pork spareribs	¼ cup Worcestershire
1 onion, stuck with cloves	¼ cup lemon juice
1 celery rib	2 teaspoons salt
1 carrot	Dash of Tabasco
2 8-ounce cans tomato sauce	1 onion, cut in thin slices
1½ cups water	1 lemon, cut in thin slices

Cut ribs into 4-rib portions. Place in large pot and cover with salted water. Add onion with cloves, celery and carrot. Bring to a boil, reduce heat and simmer, covered, 45 minutes. Meanwhile, combine tomato sauce, water, sugar, Worcestershire, lemon juice, salt and Tabasco in saucepan. Bring to a boil, reduce heat, and simmer 30 minutes. Drain ribs and pat dry with absorbent paper. Place meaty side up, in a roasting pan. Scatter onion and lemon slices over ribs and bake in 325° oven until tender, about 1 hour, basting frequently with the tomato sauce. If sauce becomes too thick, thin it with water.

Meanwhile, cook spaghetti as directed on package. Drain. Mix with 1 cup of the tomato sauce. Arrange on hot serving platter. Place ribs on top of spaghetti and serve with remaining sauce. Serves 4 to 6.

HAM BALLS WITH CRANBERRY SAUCE

8 ounces (4 cups) wide egg noodles	½ cup bread crumbs
	Dash of pepper
1 pound cooked ham, ground	2 eggs, beaten
	3 tablespoons shortening

1¼ cups and 2 tablespoons water	2 tablespoons cornstarch
¼ cup sugar	1 teaspoon grated orange rind
¼ cup brown sugar	½ cup butter, melted
1 cup cranberries	

Combine ham, bread crumbs and pepper. Mix eggs with ¼ cup water. Add to ham mixture and mix thoroughly. Shape into balls. Melt shortening in large skillet. Add ham balls and brown on all sides, about 20 minutes. Meanwhile, cook noodles as directed on package. Drain. Combine sugars and 1 cup water and bring to a boil. Add cranberries and cook until skins pop, about 5 minutes. Combine cornstarch with 2 tablespoons water and stir into cranberry mixture. Add orange rind and cook, stirring constantly, until thickened. Add ham balls and heat through. Add melted butter to hot noodles, place on heated serving platter, and pour sauce with ham balls over all. Serves 4 to 6.

HAM TETRAZZINI

8 ounces spaghetti	¼ teaspoon dry mustard
2 cups cooked ham, cut in strips	Dash of pepper
¼ cup butter	2 tablespoons dry sherry (optional)
1 small onion, chopped	1 6-ounce can sliced mushrooms, drained
¼ cup flour	
1 cup chicken broth	⅓ cup freshly grated Parmesan cheese
1 cup heavy cream	
⅓ cup shredded Gruyère or Swiss cheese	

Cook spaghetti as directed on package. Drain. In medium saucepan, sauté ham in butter about 2 minutes; remove ham. Sauté onion until crisp-tender; blend in flour. Gradually add broth and cream; cook over low heat, stirring frequently, until sauce thickens. Add Gruyère cheese, mustard, pepper and sherry; stir and heat until cheese melts. Add ham and mushrooms. Combine with spaghetti in a 2½-quart casserole or 6 individual shallow casseroles. Sprinkle Parmesan on top. If desired, also sprinkle with toasted slivered almonds. Broil 3 to 4 inches from source of heat about 4 minutes or until lightly brown. Serves 6.

HAM CASSEROLE

8 ounces straight vermicelli
2 10½-ounce cans
   condensed cream of
   chicken soup
1 cup milk
1 cup water
½ cup sliced green onions

2 tablespoons minced
   parsley
Dash of freshly ground
   pepper
2 cups diced cooked ham
¼ cup dry bread crumbs
2 tablespoons melted butter

Cook vermicelli as directed on package. Drain. In saucepan blend soup, milk and water well; stir and bring to a boil. Add onions, parsley and pepper. Toss with ham and vermicelli; turn into lightly buttered 2-quart casserole. Mix crumbs and melted butter and sprinkle over top. Bake in 350° oven 25 minutes. Serves 4 to 6.

EAST COAST RIGATONI CASSEROLE

3⅓ cups rigatoni
½ pound sausage meat
1 tablespoon cold water
1 pint oysters
¼ pound mushrooms, sliced
1 medium onion, sliced
3 tablespoons flour

Oyster liquor, plus milk to
   make 2¼ cups
½ teaspoon sage
1 teaspoon salt
Pepper
½ cup grated Cheddar
   cheese

Cook rigatoni as directed on package. Drain. Cook sausage meat with water, stirring with a fork to keep it broken up, until lightly browned. Leave sausage in pan and drain off all but about ¼ cup fat. Drain oysters, reserving oyster liquor. Chop oysters and add to sausage.

Add mushrooms and onion. Cook over low heat 10 minutes. Add flour and blend well. Gradually add milk and oyster liquor mixture, stirring constantly, and cook until thickened. Season. Fold in cooked rigatoni. Place in buttered 1½-quart casserole. Sprinkle with grated cheese. Cover and bake in 350° oven 30 minutes. Serves 4.

NOODLES WITH KRAUT-FRANKFURTER SAUCE

8 ounces (4 cups) wide egg noodles	2 to 4 tablespoons brown sugar
1 pound frankfurters, quartered	½ teaspoon salt
2 tablespoons butter	½ teaspoon basil
1 small onion, chopped	¼ teaspoon orégano
1 or 2 garlic cloves, minced	Dash of crushed red pepper
1 28-ounce can tomatoes in purée	2 cups drained sauerkraut
	¾ cup seedless raisins

In a saucepan, sauté frankfurters in butter until light brown; remove with slotted spoon. Then sauté onion and garlic until crisp-tender. Add tomatoes, brown sugar, salt, herbs, red pepper and sauerkraut. Cover and simmer 1 hour, stirring occasionally. Add frankfurters and raisins; cook over low heat 15 minutes.

Meanwhile, cook noodles as directed on package. Drain. Combine with frankfurters and sauce. Serves 4 to 6.

SPAGHETTI WITH VEAL AND PEPPERS

1 pound spaghetti	4 garlic cloves, minced
2 pounds boneless veal shoulder, cut in strips	2 19-ounce cans tomatoes
Flour	2 8-ounce cans tomato sauce
¼ cup butter	1½ to 2 teaspoons salt
⅓ cup olive oil	1½ teaspoons basil
4 medium green peppers, cut in strips	¼ to ½ teaspoon orégano
2 small onions, sliced	⅛ teaspoon freshly ground pepper

Coat veal with flour; brown in butter and oil in large skillet. Remove meat; sauté green peppers and onions about 5 minutes. Return meat; add garlic, tomatoes, tomato sauce and seasonings. Cover and simmer 1 hour, stirring occasionally. Cook spaghetti as directed on package. Drain. Serve with veal and pepper sauce. Serves 8.

NOODLES WITH VEAL BIRDS

8 ounces (4 cups) wide egg noodles
8 slices of veal scallopini (1¼ pounds)
Garlic salt, pepper and paprika
4 slices of bacon, halved
¼ cup butter
1 medium onion, chopped
½ medium green pepper, chopped
1 1-pound can tomatoes
3 tablespoons dry red wine (optional)
½ teaspoon salt
½ cup sour cream
Chopped parsley

Sprinkle veal with garlic salt, pepper and paprika; top with bacon strips. Roll up and secure with food picks. In a large skillet, brown veal birds in butter. Add onion and cook 1 minute. Mix in the green pepper, tomatoes, wine and salt. Cover and simmer 1 hour, or until meat is tender. Remove meat. Blend sauce in electric blender or force through food mill; return to skillet. Stir in sour cream. Return veal birds and heat, do not boil.

Cook noodles as directed on package. Drain. Serve with veal birds and sauce; sprinkle with parsley. Serves 4.

VEAL CASSEROLE

2 cups small shell macaroni
¼ cup flour
1 teaspoon salt
Dash of pepper
1 pound boneless veal, cut in 1-inch cubes
3 tablespoons shortening
4 cups beef broth
1 pound zucchini, sliced
1 cup julienne carrots
⅓ cup chopped onion
1 teaspoon Worcestershire

6 ounces Swiss cheese,
   sliced
¼ cup dry bread crumbs

2 tablespoons melted butter
Dash of paprika

Mix flour, salt and pepper. Dredge veal pieces with
mixture, reserving excess for later use. Heat shortening
in Dutch oven; brown meat. Add broth, cover, and
simmer 45 minutes. Add zucchini, carrots, onion and
Worcestershire. Cook 9 to 10 minutes, or until vegetables are tender. Blend reserved flour mixture with ½
cup hot broth to form a smooth paste. Add to meat and
vegetable mixture and cook until thickened, 3 to 4 minutes.

Meanwhile, cook shells as directed on package. Drain.
Place half of shells in a buttered casserole. Cover with half
of meat mixture and top with half of cheese. Repeat.
Mix crumbs with melted butter. Sprinkle over casserole
and sprinkle with paprika. Bake in 350° oven 30 minutes.
Serves 4 to 6.

SPAGHETTI WITH SAVORY VEAL STEAK

8 ounces long spaghetti
2 pounds boneless veal
   steak, 1 inch thick
¼ cup flour
1¼ teaspoons salt
   Dash of pepper
¼ cup shortening

½ cup finely chopped
   onions
1 1-pound can tomatoes
1 10½-ounce can tomato
   soup
1¼ cups warm water
   Freshly ground pepper

Cut veal into 1-inch strips. Mix flour, ¼ teaspoon salt
and pepper. Coat meat with this mixture. Melt shortening in large heavy skillet. Add meat and brown well on
all sides. Add onion, tomatoes, tomato soup, water, remaining salt and pepper to taste. Bring to boil, reduce
heat and simmer about 1 hour. Cook spaghetti as directed on package. Drain. Arrange on heated platter and
pour veal in sauce over. Serves 6.

NOODLES WITH LAMB CURRY

8 ounces (4 cups) medium
   egg noodles
2 pounds boned leg or
   shoulder of lamb, cut
   in 1-inch cubes
2 tablespoons butter
1 cup chopped onions
3 garlic cloves, chopped
3 to 4 teaspoons curry
   powder

¼ teaspoon nutmeg
3 apples, unpared, cored
   and sectioned
1 lemon, sliced
1 12½-ounce can chicken
   broth
1 teaspoon salt
   Dash of Tabasco

In Dutch oven, brown lamb in butter. Add onions, garlic, curry and nutmeg; cook 5 minutes. Stir in apples, lemon, broth, salt and Tabasco. Cover and simmer 1½ to 2 hours, or until meat is tender. Uncover; simmer to thicken sauce.

Meanwhile, cook noodles as directed on package. Drain. Serve lamb curry with noodles. Raisins, chutney, chopped nuts, flaked coconut and sour cream may be served as condiments, if desired. Serves 4 to 6.

MACARONI LUNCHEON BAKE

2½ cups elbow macaroni
1 12-ounce can luncheon
   meat, cut in strips
2 cups grated Cheddar
   cheese
½ cup chopped green
   pepper
2 tablespoons chopped
   onion

1 10½-ounce can
   condensed cream of
   mushroom soup
1 cup water
1 teaspoon salt
   Pepper

Cook macaroni as directed on package. Drain. Meanwhile, combine remaining ingredients. Add cooked macaroni; mix lightly but thoroughly. Turn into buttered 2-quart casserole. Cover. Bake in 350° oven 1 hour. Serves 6.

CREOLE SPAGHETTI BAKE

2 cups ready cut spaghetti
3 slices bacon, diced
1 small onion, chopped
1 small green pepper, chopped
1 8-ounce can tomato sauce
1 10½-ounce can condensed tomato soup

1 3- to 4-ounce can mushrooms
Salt and pepper
1 12-ounce can whole-kernel corn, drained
½ cup salad oil
½ pound Cheddar cheese, shredded

Cook spaghetti as directed on package. Drain. Sauté bacon, onion and green pepper together until bacon is crisp. Add tomato sauce, tomato soup, and mushrooms; season with salt and pepper to taste. Add corn and salad oil to cooked spaghetti, then add the sauce mixture. Turn into a 1½-quart casserole, top with shredded cheese. Bake in 350° oven until bubbly, about 30 minutes. Serves 4 to 6.

PASTA WITH POULTRY

Like pasta, chicken is appropriate to almost any occasion, from budget family meal to elegant dinner party.

Turkey is becoming more popular year around, even though it is sometimes a problem varying the big bird's third or fourth appearance. Pasta and a variety of sauces make leftover turkey delectable time and again.

Poultry and pasta are natural partners, so try these recipes and invent some variations of your own.

DIVINE TURKEY MEDLEY

4 ounces (2 cups) egg noodles
1 10½-ounce can condensed cream of mushroom soup
½ teaspoon salt
¼ teaspoon Tabasco
¼ teaspoon dry mustard

1 teaspoon curry powder
½ cup milk
½ cup shredded Cheddar cheese
2 celery ribs, sliced diagonally
4 large turkey slices or 2 cups chicken pieces

Cook noodles as directed on package. Drain. Meanwhile, in a saucepan combine soup with seasonings and milk. Place over moderate heat; bring to a boil, stirring often.

Blend in cheese. Stir in celery and noodles; mix well. Turn into 2-quart casserole. Bury turkey in noodle mixture. Bake in 350° oven until hot and bubbly, about 30 minutes. Serves 6.

TURKEY-CHEESE MELTAWAY CASSEROLE

4 ounces (1 cup) elbow
  macaroni
¼ cup butter
¼ cup finely chopped
  onion
¼ cup flour
1 teaspoon salt
  Dash of thyme
¼ teaspoon pepper

2 cups milk
1½ cups diced cooked
  turkey
4 slices Cheddar cheese
  (about 4 ounces)
½ cup bread crumbs
2 tablespoons butter,
  melted
1 teaspoon minced parsley

Cook macaroni as directed on package. Drain. Meanwhile, melt butter, add onion, and cook over low heat 3 to 5 minutes. Stir in flour, salt, thyme and pepper. Gradually add milk and cook, stirring constantly, until thickened. Arrange half of the macaroni in bottom of buttered 2-quart casserole. Put half of turkey over macaroni. Arrange cheese slices over turkey. Repeat layering once. Pour sauce over all. Mix crumbs, melted butter and parsley. Sprinkle over top of casserole. Bake in 350° oven 25 minutes. Serves 4.

BIT-OF-TURKEY CASSEROLE

8 ounces (2 cups) elbow
  macaroni
1 cup sour cream
1 cup milk
2 eggs, slightly beaten
½ teaspoon salt

¼ cup flour
2 tablespoons lemon juice
1½ cups cooked broccoli
  pieces
2 cups cooked diced turkey
  (or chicken)

Cook macaroni as directed on package. Drain. Meanwhile, in top of double boiler, combine sour cream, milk, eggs, salt and flour. Cook over boiling water, stirring occasionally until mixture begins to thicken. Stir in lemon juice. Combine sauce, macaroni, broccoli and turkey. Turn into buttered 2-quart casserole. Cover and bake in 350° oven about 15 minutes. Serves 4 to 6.

APPLE-RAISIN STUFFING FOR POULTRY

6 ounces (3 cups) medium egg noodles
½ cup butter
½ cup chopped celery
1 teaspoon salt
Freshly ground pepper

3 cups chopped unpeeled apples
1 cup raisins
½ cup soft bread crumbs
½ cup chicken broth

Cook noodles as directed on package. Drain. Melt butter; add celery, and cook about 5 minutes, stirring frequently. Combine with noodles, mixing well. Add salt, pepper to taste, apples, raisins and bread crumbs. Mix lightly. Stir in broth. Use to stuff a small turkey or a large chicken.

FRICASSEED CHICKEN WITH SPAGHETTI

8 ounces spaghetti
1 frying chicken (cut in serving pieces)
Seasoned flour
2 tablespoons salad oil

1 chicken bouillon cube
1 cup hot water
½ teaspoon salt
⅛ teaspoon pepper
1 3-ounce can mushrooms

Roll chicken in seasoned flour; brown in hot oil. Dissolve bouillon cube in hot water; add to browned chicken. Season with salt and pepper. Add mushrooms with liquid. Cover and simmer until chicken is tender and sauce slightly thickened, about 45 minutes. Cook spaghetti as directed on package. Drain. Arrange on platter with chicken on top. Pour pan gravy over chicken. Serves 4.

CHICKEN TETRAZZINI

8 ounces spaghetti	Dash of white pepper
¼ cup butter	1 6-ounce can sliced
¼ cup flour	mushrooms, drained
1 cup chicken broth	2½ to 3 cups diced cooked
1 cup heavy cream	chicken
⅓ cup shredded Gruyère	⅓ cup freshly grated
or Swiss cheese	Parmesan cheese
2 tablespoons sherry	
(optional)	

Cook spaghetti according to package directions. Drain. Melt butter in large saucepan; blend in flour. Gradually add broth and cream. Cook over low heat, stirring constantly, until sauce thickens. Mix in cheese, sherry and pepper; heat and stir until cheese melts; add mushrooms. Remove from heat and stir in chicken. Add spaghetti to the sauce. Turn into 2-quart shallow flameproof casserole. Sprinkle Parmesan cheese on top. Broil 3 to 4 inches from source of heat 5 to 7 minutes or until light brown. Serve immediately. Serves 6 to 8.

DOWN-SOUTH STEW

8 ounces (2 cups) elbow	1 cup cooked or canned
macaroni	tomatoes
1 stewing chicken, cut up	Dash of pepper
6 teaspoons salt	1 teaspoon Worcestershire
1 small onion, chopped	1 cup cooked okra
2 cups whole-kernel corn	

Place chicken in a large kettle, cover with water, and add 4 teaspoons of the salt and the onion. Bring to a boil, reduce heat and simmer, covered, until tender, about 1 hour and 45 minutes. Remove chicken from broth and cool. Remove chicken from bones and cut into pieces. Put bones back into broth and boil broth down to about

2 quarts. Skim fat from surface and strain the broth. Put back into kettle, add corn, tomatoes, remaining 2 teaspoons salt, pepper and Worcestershire. Simmer 15 minutes, stirring occasionally. Add macaroni and cook about 10 minutes longer, or until macaroni is *al dente*. Put 2 cups of the cut-up chicken into the stew with the okra and heat thoroughly. Serves 6.

CHICKEN-RIPPLET CASSEROLE

2 cups ripplet egg noodles
2 teaspoons butter
2 teaspoons flour
½ cup cream, scalded
8 ounces cream cheese, softened
1 cup hot chicken stock
2 cups diced cooked chicken
3 tablespoons diced pimiento
3 tablespoons chopped ripe olives
Salt and pepper

Cook ripplets as directed on package. Drain. Melt butter and stir in flour smoothly. Add cream and cook, stirring constantly, until thickened. Beat cheese into sauce until smooth. Add stock and mix well. Add chicken, pimiento, olives and noodles, and blend well. Season to taste with salt and pepper. Pour into buttered casserole and bake in 350° oven 30 minutes. Serves 6.

CHICKEN PAPRIKA

8 ounces (4 cups) medium egg noodles
3 tablespoons butter
1 large onion, sliced and separated into rings
¼ cup flour
2 tablespoons paprika
1 teaspoon salt
¼ teaspoon pepper
2 cups chicken stock
1 cup sour cream
3 cups diced cooked chicken

Melt butter. Add onion and sauté until transparent. Combine flour, paprika, salt and pepper and stir into onion smoothly. Gradually add chicken stock, cook, stirring constantly, until thickened. Meanwhile, cook noodles as directed on package. Drain. Add sour cream to sauce, mixing well, and heat, but do not boil. Stir chicken into sauce. Fold in noodles so that they are all well coated with sauce. Serves 6.

SPAGHETTI WITH RICH SAUCE

8 ounces thin spaghetti	1 cup shelled peas
½ cup butter	¼ pound mushrooms, diced
½ cup slivered prosciutto	1 1-pound can tomatoes
½ cup slivered cooked chicken	Salt, pepper and cayenne
¼ cup dry white wine	1 cup freshly grated Parmesan cheese

Melt butter. Add prosciutto and brown lightly. Add chicken and wine and simmer gently until wine starts to boil. Add peas, mushrooms and tomatoes and cook at a simmer, stirring occasionally, until peas are done and sauce has thickened slightly. Season to taste. Meanwhile, cook spaghetti as directed on package. Drain. Mix well with sauce and cheese. Serves 4.

CHICKEN MARENGO WITH NOODLES

8 ounces (4 cups) medium egg noodles	12 medium mushrooms
2 broiler-fryers, 2½ pounds each, cut in serving pieces	1 garlic clove, finely chopped
	2 tablespoons flour
	½ cup water
½ cup seasoned flour	3 tablespoons dry sherry (optional)
⅓ cup olive oil	
¼ cup butter	4 medium tomatoes, peeled and quartered
12 small white onions, cooked	Salt

Coat chicken pieces lightly with seasoned flour. Cook in oil over medium heat until browned on all sides. Cover and cook over low heat 40 minutes, or until tender.

Meanwhile, melt butter. Add onions, mushrooms and garlic; cover and cook 10 minutes, stirring occasionally. Blend in 2 tablespoons flour. Gradually add water and sherry; cook over low heat, stirring constantly, until thickened. Add tomatoes and salt to taste. Cover, and cook 10 minutes, stirring occasionally. Meanwhile, cook noodles as directed on package. Drain. Arrange on serving platter and top with chicken and sauce. Garnish with parsley, if desired. Serves 6.

SPAGHETTI ROYALE

8 ounces spaghetti	¼ cup flour
¼ cup butter	1½ teaspoons salt
¼ pound mushrooms, sliced	2½ cups chicken stock
1 medium onion, chopped	2 cups diced cooked
1 small green pepper, cut in strips	chicken
	1 4-ounce can pimientos,
1 tablespoon chopped parsley	drained and diced
	1 tablespoon lemon juice
½ teaspoon thyme	

Melt butter in saucepan. Add mushrooms, onion, green pepper, parsley and thyme and cook until vegetables are tender. Blend in flour and salt. Gradually add chicken stock and cook, stirring constantly, until thickened and boiling. Add chicken, pimientos and lemon juice. Stir and heat to serving temperature. Meanwhile, cook spaghetti as directed on package. Drain. To serve, toss with chicken mixture. Serves 4.

CHICKEN KALAKAUA

2 cups elbow macaroni	1 quart chicken broth
2 medium onions, chopped	2½ cups diced cooked
1 green pepper, chopped	chicken
¼ cup olive oil	1 20-ounce can cream-
1 small garlic clove, minced	style corn

2 8-ounce cans tomato
   sauce
2½ teaspoons chili powder
2 4-ounce cans mushrooms,
   drained

1½ teaspoons salt
½ cup grated Parmesan
   cheese
¼ cup butter

Cook macaroni as directed on package. Drain. Meanwhile, sauté onions and green pepper in oil. Do not brown. Add garlic. Then combine with macaroni, chicken broth, chicken, corn, tomato sauce, chili powder, mushrooms and salt. Bring to simmering point. Place in buttered 2-quart casserole. Top with cheese and dot with butter. Bake in 350° oven until top is delicately brown, about 25 minutes. Serves 4 to 6.

CHICKEN BREASTS WITH CREAMY NOODLES

8 ounces (4 cups) wide egg
   noodles
½ cup flour
2 teaspoons salt
¼ teaspoon pepper
¼ teaspoon poultry
   seasoning

3 chicken breasts, halved
⅓ cup salad oil
1 cup sour cream
¼ teaspoon onion powder
¼ cup milk
3 tablespoons snipped
   chives

Combine flour, 1½ teaspoons salt, pepper and poultry seasoning. Coat chicken pieces with the mixture. Heat oil in a large heavy skillet. Add chicken and brown well on all sides. Cover and reduce heat. Cook until chicken is tender, 20 to 25 minutes. Meanwhile, cook noodles as directed on package. Drain. Combine with sour cream, onion powder, ½ teaspoon salt, milk and chives. Serve with chicken pieces on top. Serves 6.

SPAGHETTI AND CHICKEN SKILLET

8 ounces spaghetti
½ cup butter

1 broiler-fryer, 2½ pounds,
   cut in serving pieces

½ cup boiling water
1 10½-ounce can
    condensed cream of
    chicken soup

1 1-pound can small
    whole carrots, drained
1 medium green pepper, cut
    into rings
½ cup sliced stuffed olives

Cook spaghetti according to directions. Drain. Heat butter in skillet. Add chicken and cook until browned on all sides. Remove chicken. Drain off drippings, reserving 2 tablespoons drippings. Add ½ cup boiling water and reserved drippings to skillet. Heat to boiling, stirring occasionally. Add soup and stir until blended. Add spaghetti with remaining ingredients and heat to serving temperature over low heat, stirring occasionally. Serves 4 to 6. (This dish illustrated in color section.)

MEATLESS PASTA DISHES

Seafood and cheese, the basic alternatives to meat, deserve a special place in pasta cookery. These recipes make meatless meal planning a breeze.

NOODLES ALFREDO

2 pounds (16 cups) medium egg noodles

1 pound sweet butter, softened

4 cups freshly grated Parmesan cheese

1 cup heavy cream at room temperature

Cook noodles as directed on package. Drain. Place butter in hot 4-quart casserole; add noodles and toss gently. Add cheese and toss again. Pour in cream; toss. Sprinkle with freshly ground pepper if desired. Serves 12 to 16. (This dish illustrated in color section.)

CHEESE MANICOTTI

4 ounces (7 pieces) manicotti

1 pound ricotta or cottage cheese

1 cup (4 ounces) shredded mozzarella cheese

3 eggs, beaten

1 teaspoon parsley flakes

¼ teaspoon seasoned salt
⅛ teaspoon pepper

1 10¾-ounce can
   condensed Cheddar
   cheese soup, heated

Cook manicotti as directed on package. Drain. Cool. Blend together ricotta and mozzarella cheeses, eggs, parsley flakes, seasoned salt and pepper. Stuff manicotti with cheese filling; place in buttered baking dish. Pour soup over manicotti. Bake in 400° oven 25 minutes. Serves 4.

NOODLES BUDAPEST

8 ounces (4 cups) wide egg
   noodles
2 cups sour cream
8 ounces creamed cottage
   cheese
1 medium onion, finely
   chopped

1 garlic clove, minced
½ teaspoon salt
   Dash of Tabasco
1 teaspoon Worcestershire
   Paprika

Cook noodles as directed on package. Drain. Combine noodles, sour cream, cottage cheese, onion, garlic, salt, Tabasco and Worcestershire; mix well. Turn into a 1½-quart casserole; sprinkle with paprika. Bake in 350° oven 30 to 45 minutes. Sprinkle noodles with additional paprika. Serves 4 to 6.

RIPPLETS WITH THREE CHEESES

12 ounces (6 cups) ripplet
    egg noodles
    Fine dry bread crumbs
 2 tablespoons butter
 1 cup freshly grated
    Parmesan cheese

1 cup diced Swiss cheese
1 cup diced mozzarella
   cheese
3 cups Thin White Sauce
   (see next page)

Cook ripplets as directed on package. Drain. Meanwhile, coat a buttered shallow 3-quart baking dish with bread crumbs. Toss ripplets with butter, then with Parmesan cheese. Add Swiss and mozzarella cheeses; toss lightly. Turn half of noodle mixture into prepared dish; top with half of white sauce. Repeat layers. Sprinkle grated Parmesan cheese or bread crumbs on top, if desired. Bake in 350° oven 25 minutes. Serves 6.

Thin White Sauce: Melt 3 tablespoons butter in a saucepan; blend in 3 tablespoons flour. Gradually add 3 cups milk; cook, stirring constantly, until sauce boils 1 minute. Add 1½ teaspoons salt, ¼ teaspoon pepper and ⅛ teaspoon nutmeg. Makes 3 cups.

NOODLE CHEESE RING

8 ounces (4 cups) fine egg
   noodles
3 tablespoons butter
3 tablespoons flour
½ teaspoon salt
⅛ teaspoon pepper
1 cup milk

½ cup heavy cream
3 eggs, separated
½ pound Cheddar cheese,
   grated
2 tablespoons fine dry
   bread crumbs

Cook noodles as directed on package. Drain. Meanwhile, melt butter in a saucepan; blend in flour, salt and pepper. Slowly add milk and cream; stir and cook until sauce thickens. Beat egg yolks; stir in some of hot sauce; return yolk mixture to saucepan. Stir and cook over low heat 3 minutes. Remove from heat; stir in cheese until melted; chill.

Beat egg whites until stiff; fold into cheese sauce along with cooked noodles. Sprinkle crumbs over bottom of well-buttered 6½-cup ring mold. Spoon in noodle mixture. Set mold in pan of hot water. Bake in 350° oven 1 hour, or until a knife inserted comes out clean. Remove from water; let stand 5 minutes. Unmold. Fill center with green vegetable if desired. Serves 6.

CHEDDAR NOODLE CASSEROLE

8 ounces (4 cups) wide egg
    noodles
1 cup sliced celery
¼ cup chopped onion
¼ cup butter
¼ cup flour
1 teaspoon salt
1 teaspoon chervil

⅛ to ¼ teaspoon pepper
1 teaspoon Worcestershire
3 cups milk
8 ounces Cheddar cheese,
    grated (about 2 cups)
1 cup drained sauerkraut
¾ cup raisins

Cook noodles as directed on package. Drain. Meanwhile, sauté celery and onion in butter until almost tender; mix in flour, salt, chervil, pepper and Worcestershire. Gradually stir in milk; cook, stirring constantly, until sauce boils 1 minute. Add 1½ cups of the Cheddar cheese and the sauerkraut; stir and heat until cheese melts. Combine with noodles and raisins in 2-quart casserole. Sprinkle remaining cheese on top. Bake in 375° oven 20 minutes. Serves 4 to 6.

MOSTACCIOLI CHEESE CASSEROLE

12 ounces mostaccioli
½ pound process American
    cheese, cubed
2 tablespoons butter
2 tablespoons flour

1 teaspoon salt
⅛ teaspoon pepper
2½ cups milk
⅓ cup fine dry bread
    crumbs

Cook mostaccioli as directed on package. Drain. Add cheese cubes to cooked mostaccioli and turn into buttered 2½-quart casserole. Melt butter in saucepan; blend in flour, salt and pepper. Gradually add milk; cook, stirring constantly, until slightly thickened. Pour over mostaccioli and cheese. Sprinkle bread crumbs over top and bake in 350° oven for 30 to 45 minutes, or until mixture is bubbly. Serves 6.

MARVELOUS MACARONI AND CHEESE WITH VARIATIONS

8 ounces (2 cups) elbow macaroni	1¼ teaspoons salt
¼ cup chopped onion	½ teaspoon dry mustard
3 tablespoons butter	¼ teaspoon pepper
3 tablespoons flour	1 teaspoon Worcestershire
3 cups milk	2½ cups grated sharp Cheddar cheese

Cook macaroni as directed on package. Drain. Meanwhile, cook onion in butter until crisp-tender. Quickly stir in flour. Gradually add milk, stirring constantly; add seasonings. Cook, stirring, until sauce boils 1 minute. Stir in 2 cups of the cheese; continue stirring until cheese melts. Remove sauce from heat; combine with macaroni. Turn into 1½-quart casserole. Sprinkle with remaining ½ cup cheese. Bake in 375° oven 20 minutes, or until bubbling and lightly browned. Garnish with parsley, if desired. Serves 4.

VARIATIONS:
1. Add ¼ cup chopped or sliced olives to cheese sauce.
2. Add 1 3- or 4-ounce can chopped or sliced mushrooms, drained, to cheese sauce.
3. Add ½ cup chopped green pepper to cheese sauce.
4. Add 1 4-ounce can or jar pimientos, drained and diced, to cheese sauce.
5. Add 2 tablespoons chopped chives to cheese sauce.
6. Add 1½ tablespoons caraway seeds to cheese sauce.
7. Add 2 tablespoons poppy seeds to cheese sauce.
8. Top macaroni and cheese with 2 medium tomatoes, sliced, before baking.

MACARONI SUPREMO

8 ounces elbow macaroni	3 tablespoons flour
3 tablespoons butter	½ teaspoon salt

⅛ teaspoon pepper
⅛ teaspoon paprika
2½ cups milk

2 cups grated Cheddar
cheese

Cook macaroni as directed on package. Drain. Meanwhile, melt butter; blend in flour, salt, pepper and paprika. Gradually add milk; cook, stirring constantly until thickened. Add two-thirds of the cheese and stir until cheese is melted. Turn macaroni into a well-buttered 2-quart casserole. Stir in sauce. Sprinkle remaining cheese on top. Bake in 375° oven about 30 minutes, or until delicately browned. Serves 4 to 6.

VERMICELLI PARMESAN

12 ounces vermicelli
⅓ cup butter
2½ cups shredded Cheddar
cheese

1 cup milk
⅓ cup grated Parmesan
cheese
Paprika

Cook vermicelli as directed on package. Drain. Add butter and toss to coat vermicelli. Turn into a buttered 3-quart casserole. Add Cheddar cheese and milk; cover and heat in 350° oven for about 25 minutes, or until cheese is melted. Stir lightly and sprinkle Parmesan cheese on top. Garnish with paprika. Serves 6.

CREAMY EGG AND MACARONI BAKE

4 ounces (1 cup) elbow
macaroni
1 10½-ounce can condensed
cream of celery soup
¾ cup milk
2 tablespoons finely
chopped green pepper

1 tablespoon minced onion
1 teaspoon Worcestershire
½ teaspoon salt
4 hard-cooked eggs, sliced
Buttered bread crumbs
Grated Parmesan cheese

Cook macaroni as directed on package. Drain. Meanwhile, in a saucepan, combine soup, milk, green pepper, onion, Worcestershire and salt. Stir and heat to piping hot. Arrange a layer of egg slices in bottom of buttered 1½-quart casserole. Cover with a layer of macaroni. Repeat layering twice. Pour soup mixture over all. Combine buttered crumbs and cheese. Sprinkle over top of casserole. Bake in 350° oven about 20 minutes. Serves 4.

SPANISH LOAF

8 ounces (2 cups) elbow macaroni	1 cup soft bread crumbs
1 8-ounce can tomato sauce with mushrooms	2 eggs, well beaten
½ cup milk	⅓ cup sliced ripe olives
2 tablespoons salad oil	2 tablespoons finely chopped green pepper
2 cups shredded Cheddar cheese	2 tablespoons minced onion
	1 teaspoon salt
	1 teaspoon chili powder

Cook macaroni as directed on package. Drain. Combine with remaining ingredients and pour into well-buttered loaf pan (9x5x3 inches). Bake in 325° oven 30 to 35 minutes. Unmold on platter; cut in slices. Serves 6.

MUSHROOM SPAGHETTINI

8 ounces spaghettini	¼ pound sweet butter, cut into chunks and at room temperature
1 3-ounce can chopped broiled mushrooms, undrained and heated to serving temperature	¼ pound Parmesan cheese, freshly grated

Cook spaghettini as directed on package. Drain. Working rapidly, return spaghettini to kettle with undrained mushrooms, butter and cheese. Stir vigorously with a tossing motion until mixture is creamy in appearance. Serve immediately and pass the pepper mill. Serves 4.

NOODLES WITH FLOUNDER ROLL-UPS

8 ounces (4 cups) medium
  egg noodles
2 pounds flounder fillets
  Seasoned salt
1 cup bread cubes
½ cup grated Cheddar
  cheese

2 tablespoons chopped
  parsley
¼ cup butter, melted
2 tablespoons lemon juice
  Chopped parsley

Sprinkle flounder fillets with seasoned salt. Combine bread cubes, cheese and parsley; place some on center of each fillet. Roll up and secure with food picks. Place in buttered shallow baking dish. Sprinkle with butter and lemon juice. Bake in 350° oven 25 minutes, or until fish flakes when tested with a fork.

Meanwhile, cook noodles as directed on package. Drain. Turn onto serving plate; sprinkle with chopped parsley. Arrange flounder roll-ups on top and pour fish pan juices over all. Serves 6.

SUNDAY SUPPER RING

1 pound (8 cups) wide egg
  noodles
½ cup butter
½ cup flour
½ teaspoon salt
1 teaspoon dry mustard
1 teaspoon paprika
3½ cups milk

3 cups grated Cheddar
  cheese (about 12
  ounces)
½ cup sherry (or apple
  cider)
3 10-ounce packages
  frozen Brussels sprouts

Cook noodles according to package directions. Drain (but do *not* rinse). Turn into oiled 9-inch ring mold (8-cup capacity). Cover and keep warm; allow about 10 minutes for the noodles to set in ring-shape. Meanwhile, melt butter in saucepan; blend in flour, salt, dry mustard and paprika. Gradually add milk and cook, stirring constantly, until mixture thickens. Add cheese, stir until melted. Add sherry and heat to serving temperature. Keep cheese sauce warm. Cook Brussels sprouts according to package directions. Drain, if necessary.

Loosen noodles with spatula and invert mold onto serving plate. Fill center with hot cooked Brussels sprouts. Pour cheese sauce over Brussels sprouts and noodles; serve with remaining cheese sauce. Serves 8. (This dish illustrated in color section.)

SEAFARER'S PASTA

8 ounces spaghetti
⅓ cup sliced pitted ripe olives
1 8-ounce can minced clams, undrained
1 6½- or 7-ounce can chunk-style tuna, drained
¼ cup chopped green pepper
1 1½-ounce package spaghetti sauce mix
1 6-ounce can tomato paste

Cook spaghetti as directed on package. Drain. Meanwhile, heat olive slices with undrained clams, tuna and green pepper in spaghetti sauce mix prepared with tomato paste as directed on sauce mix package. Arrange spaghetti on heated platter and pour sauce over. Serves 4.

CREAMY RIGATONI CASSEROLE

4 cups rigatoni
1 cup creamed cottage cheese
1 cup sour cream
1 7½-ounce can chopped clams
¼ cup finely chopped onion
½ teaspoon Worcestershire
1 tablespoon chopped chives
Dash of Tabasco
1 teaspoon salt
¼ teaspoon minced garlic
½ cup grated Cheddar cheese

Cook rigatoni as directed on package. Drain. Combine cottage cheese, sour cream, clams with juice, onion, Worcestershire, chives, Tabasco, salt and garlic; mix well. Fold in rigatoni. Place in buttered casserole. Top with grated cheese. Bake in 350° oven 30 minutes. Serves 4 to 6.

SALMON DUMPLING CASSEROLE

4 cups dumplings
¼ cup and 3 tablespoons melted butter
¼ cup flour
2 cups milk
1 egg yolk
Salt and pepper
1 15½-ounce can salmon, drained and flaked
½ cup dry bread crumbs

Cook dumplings as directed on package. Drain. Arrange on bottom and sides of a baking dish, leaving a depression in center for the salmon. Heat ¼ cup of the butter and blend in flour smoothly. Add milk and cook, stirring constantly, until sauce is thick and smooth. Beat a little of the sauce with the egg yolk, return to sauce, and stir to blend. Season. Stir in salmon and pour into center of dumpling-lined dish. Mix bread crumbs with remaining melted butter and sprinkle over casserole. Bake in 400° oven until nicely browned, about 20 minutes. Serves 4 to 6.

NOODLE-SALMON SCALLOP

8 ounces (4 cups) medium egg noodles
4 tablespoons melted butter
2 tablespoons flour
1 teaspoon salt
¼ teaspoon pepper
1½ cups milk
1 to 2 tablespoons lemon juice
1 7¾-ounce can salmon, flaked
⅓ cup chopped almonds
½ cup cracker crumbs

Cook noodles as directed on package. Drain. Heat 2 tablespoons butter and stir in flour and seasonings smoothly. Add milk and cook, stirring constantly, until thickened. Sprinkle lemon juice on flaked salmon. Mix with cooked noodles, almonds and sauce. Turn into a shallow 1½-quart baking dish. Mix cracker crumbs with remaining butter and sprinkle over the top. Bake in 350° oven 20 to 25 minutes. Serves 4.

MACARONI-SHRIMP CURRY

8 ounces (2 cups) elbow macaroni
1 teaspoon salt
1 tablespoon curry powder
¼ teaspoon pepper
½ cup seedless white raisins
½ cup flaked coconut
½ cup chopped walnuts

½ cup chopped onion
½ cup chopped red apple
1 pound cooked cleaned shrimps, diced
1 10½-ounce can condensed cream of celery soup
¾ cup water

Cook macaroni as directed on package. Drain. Add salt, curry powder, pepper, raisins, coconut, walnuts, onion, apple and shrimps; toss lightly. Blend soup and water. Pour over shrimp mixture and blend carefully. Pour into buttered 2-quart casserole. Bake in 350° oven 25 to 30 minutes, or until lightly browned and bubbly. Serves 4 to 6.

NOTE: It's fun to serve condiments with this dish; chutney, toasted flaked coconut, chopped peanuts, chopped hard-cooked egg, chopped green pepper—any or all, but don't leave out the chutney.

TUNA TETRAZZINI

8 ounces Italian style spaghetti
¼ cup butter
¼ cup flour
1 cup chicken broth
1 cup heavy cream
⅓ cup shredded Gruyère or Swiss cheese

2 tablespoons dry sherry (optional)
2 6½- or 7-ounce cans tuna, drained
1 3-ounce can chopped mushrooms
Salt and white pepper
⅓ cup grated Parmesan cheese

Cook spaghetti as directed on package. Drain. In medium saucepan, melt butter; blend in flour. Gradually add broth and cream; cook over low heat, stirring frequently, until sauce thickens. Add Gruyère cheese and sherry; stir and heat until cheese melts. Add tuna, mushrooms and salt and pepper to taste. Combine with spaghetti in shallow 1½-quart baking dish. Sprinkle Parmesan on top. If desired, also sprinkle with toasted slivered almonds.

Broil in preheated broiler 3 to 4 inches from source of heat 4 minutes, or until lightly brown. Serves 6.

EGG NOODLES WITH CREAMED TUNA

8 ounces (4 cups) medium egg noodles

1 1-pound can green peas, undrained

1 6-ounce can mushroom caps, undrained

Milk

¼ cup butter

¼ cup flour

2 teaspoons instant minced onion

2 teaspoons salt

¼ teaspoon pepper

2 6½- or 7-ounce cans chunk-style tuna, drained

2 tablespoons chopped pimiento

Cook noodles as directed on package. Drain. Meanwhile, drain liquids from peas and mushrooms into measuring cup; add enough milk to measure 3 cups. Set aside. Melt butter in saucepan; quickly blend in flour, onion and seasonings. Gradually stir in milk mixture. Bring to a boil, stirring constantly; boil 1 minute. Stir in tuna, vegetables and pimiento; heat to serving temperature. Serve over noodles. Serves 4.

SAUCES FOR PASTA

Although some of these recipes may take you a little more time to prepare than opening and heating a can of commercial sauce, a homemade pasta sauce is well worth the effort. If you have the impression that all pasta sauces contain tomato, there are recipes in this section that do not, and these are among the most delicious of all. Once you've learned to make a perfect sauce, one with a delicate subtle flavor, you are well on your way to mastering the art of Italian cooking.

The art is in using good ingredients and going as lightly as possible on the olive oil and garlic so as not to overwhelm either the other ingredients or the pasta—or your family!

There's a marvelous way to save time, in a sense, when you prepare one of the longer-cooking recipes in the following group: double the recipe, use half of it today, and freeze the rest for another meal. Remove frozen sauce from the freezer about 2 hours ahead of time and thaw it enough to slide easily out of the container. Heat gently to serving temperature while the pasta is cooking.

BASIC TOMATO SAUCE

3 slices bacon, diced	2 10½-ounce cans
1 tablespoon olive or salad	condensed beef broth
oil	½ teaspoon salt
½ cup finely chopped onion	¼ teaspoon sugar
½ cup finely chopped celery	2 garlic cloves, crushed
½ cup finely chopped	8 parsley sprigs
carrots	½ teaspoon thyme
2 28-ounce cans tomatoes in	1 bay leaf
tomato purée	

Cook bacon in oil in a large saucepan or Dutch oven over low heat about 2 minutes. Add onion, celery and carrot and cook until onion is tender. Add tomatoes and break up with the back of a spoon. Stir in remaining ingredients and simmer uncovered 2 hours, stirring occasionally. Add a little water during cooking if sauce becomes too thick. Strain sauce through a sieve or force through a food mill. Use with all pasta products. Makes about 1 quart.

TABASCO TOMATO SAUCE *

2 tablespoons olive oil	½ cup dry red wine
1 pound ground beef	(optional)
2 medium onions, chopped	2 teaspoons salt
1 garlic clove, minced	1 bay leaf
1 3-ounce can mushrooms	Dash of thyme
1 1-pound can tomatoes	½ teaspoon Tabasco
1 6-ounce can tomato paste	1 teaspoon Worcestershire

Heat oil in a heavy saucepan. Add meat, breaking it up into small pieces with a fork. Add onions and garlic; when meat is browned, stir in mushrooms with liquid

---

* This sauce is particularly suitable for freezing.

and remaining ingredients. Simmer until sauce is thickened, about 30 minutes. Enough for 1 pound of pasta.

ITALIAN-STYLE TOMATO SAUCE

1 large onion, chopped
3 tablespoons olive oil
1 6-ounce can tomato paste
1 teaspoon parsley flakes
1 teaspoon sugar
⅛ teaspoon pepper

2 cups tomato juice, or
   juice from 28-ounce
   can of tomatoes plus
   water to make 2 cups
1 teaspoon orégano
2 teaspoons salt

Sauté onion in oil until transparent. Add remaining ingredients and blend well; simmer over low heat for 8 to 10 minutes. Makes about 2½ cups.

SEAFOOD SAUCE

1 garlic clove
½ cup butter
½ cup chicken broth
½ cup chablis or dry white
   wine
¼ cup chopped parsley
¼ teaspoon basil
¼ teaspoon orégano

1 7½-ounce can crab meat,
   drained and boned
1 5-ounce can lobster,
   drained and boned
2 4½-ounce cans shrimps,
   drained, rinsed and
   chopped
Salt and pepper

Sauté garlic in butter until golden; discard garlic. Add broth, wine, parsley and herbs to butter; bring to simmering point. Drain crab meat and lobster and discard bony tissue. Break seafood into pieces and add to sauce with salt and pepper to taste. Heat slowly to serving temperature. Enough for 1 pound of pasta.

TUNA CHEESE SAUCE

¼ cup butter
¼ cup flour
½ teaspoon salt
¼ teaspoon pepper
½ teaspoon thyme
½ teaspoon parsley flakes

2 cups milk
2 cups grated Cheddar
   cheese
1 7-ounce can tuna, drained
   and flaked

Melt butter. Blend in flour and seasonings and cook, stirring constantly, until smooth and bubbly. Gradually stir in milk. Bring to a boil, stirring constantly, and boil 1 minute. Remove from heat, mix in cheese and tuna and stir until cheese is melted. Enough for 8 ounces of pasta.

SEVEN-WAY SAUCE

1 pound lean beef, ground *
1 cup chopped onion
2 tablespoons olive oil
2 8-ounce cans tomato sauce

Salt and pepper
1 teaspoon Italian seasoning
1 cup grated Cheddar cheese

Cook beef and onion in oil until browned. Add tomato sauce, salt and pepper to taste and Italian seasoning. Cover and simmer 15 minutes. Mix in cheese when ready to serve. Enough for 8 ounces of pasta.

* For ground beef you may substitute diced cooked ham, sliced frankfurters, bologna cubes, sliced cooked sausage, diced cooked chicken or tuna. Add the substitute to browned onion with tomato sauce and seasonings.

RAGU BOLOGNESE **

¼ pound salt pork, chopped
1 pound ground beef chuck
¼ pound ground lean veal
1 medium onion, thinly sliced
1 carrot, thinly sliced
1 celery rib, diced
1 whole clove
1 cup beef stock
1 tablespoon tomato paste

½ teaspoon salt
Freshly ground pepper
1 cup water
¼ pound mushrooms, coarsely chopped
4 chicken livers, coarsely chopped
½ cup heavy cream

Put salt pork into a deep skillet and fry until brown. Pour off some of the fat. Put in beef, veal, onion, carrot, celery and the clove and brown well over low heat.

** This sauce is particularly suitable for freezing.

Add stock; simmer till stock evaporates, about 45 minutes. Add tomato paste, salt, pepper to taste and water. Cover pan and cook over low heat 1 hour. Add mushrooms and chicken livers and cook 15 minutes longer. Just before serving add cream and heat through. (Do not add cream if you plan to freeze the sauce.) Use in lasagne and as a sauce for spaghetti, ravioli and cannelloni. Makes about 3 cups.

MEAT-MUSHROOM SAUCE *

2 ounces salt pork
1 pound ground beef chuck
2 garlic cloves, crushed
½ cup dry white wine
½ pound mushrooms, quartered
2 celery ribs, sliced
¼ teaspoon rosemary
1 teaspoon basil
1 tablespoon minced parsley
Dash of cinnamon
4 medium tomatoes, peeled and diced
1 8-ounce can tomato sauce
Salt and pepper
1 teaspoon sugar

Dice pork and fry to get out all fat. Discard cracklings. Add beef and cook, stirring with a fork, until it browns slightly and loses all red color. Add garlic and cook until golden brown. Add wine and cook 10 minutes. Add remaining ingredients. Simmer gently 1 hour, stirring frequently. Enough for 1 pound of pasta.

* This sauce is particularly suitable for freezing.

"RED HOT" FRANK SAUCE

3 tablespoons butter
½ cup chopped onion
1 garlic clove, minced
1 pound frankfurters, sliced diagonally
3 tablespoons chopped parsley
1 1-pound can tomatoes
1 6-ounce can tomato paste
⅛ to ¼ teaspoon crushed red pepper
1 teaspoon salt
¼ teaspoon orégano

Melt butter in a large skillet and add onion, garlic and frankfurters; cook over medium heat until frankfurters are browned. Add remaining ingredients. Mix well and cook, uncovered, over medium heat for 20 minutes. Cover and continue cooking 20 minutes longer. Enough for 8 ounces of pasta.

SAUSAGE SAUCE

1 pound Italian hot sausage, cut in 1-inch pieces
1 pound Italian sweet sausage, cut in 1-inch pieces
1½ cups water
1 cup diced green pepper
½ cup chopped onion
3 8-ounce cans tomato sauce
1 6-ounce can tomato paste
Salt and pepper

In a large saucepan, simmer sausages in ½ cup water, covered, for 10 minutes. Uncover and simmer until juices cook down and sausage is browned, stirring occasionally. Using a slotted spoon, remove sausage and discard all but 1 tablespoon drippings. In same saucepan, sauté green pepper and onion until crisp-tender. Add tomato sauce, tomato paste, remaining 1 cup water and salt and pepper to taste. Return sausage; simmer covered 30 minutes, stirring occasionally. Enough for 1 pound of pasta.

ANCHOVY SAUCE

¼ cup olive oil
½ cup chopped onion
2 garlic cloves, crushed
½ teaspoon basil
1 2-ounce can anchovies, drained
1 cup chopped parsley

Combine oil, onion, garlic and basil; cook over low heat 15 minutes. Mash anchovies and add to onion mixture; continue cooking about 3 minutes. Add parsley. Enough for 8 ounces of pasta.

SAUCE VERDE

1 cup firmly packed spinach leaves	2 tablespoons chopped walnuts
1 cup firmly packed parsley leaves	¼ cup freshly grated Romano cheese
1 small garlic clove	¼ cup freshly grated Parmesan cheese
¼ cup butter	¾ to 1 teaspoon salt
¼ cup olive oil	½ teaspoon basil
¼ cup pine nuts (optional)	

Wash spinach and parsley; shake to remove excess water, but allow moisture to cling to leaves. Place with remaining ingredients in electric blender. Blend at high speed until mixture looks like a thick purée but with some specks of spinach and parsley still visible. If sauce seems too thick, add small amount of water. Toss with pasta until completely coated. Enough for 1 pound of pasta.

SNACKS, APPETIZERS AND
SIDE DISHES

When you are searching for something exciting to serve with beverages at your next party, don't forget appetizers made of pasta.

These should be made in rather small portions. They will charm your guests.

Buttered pasta in any form makes a delicious side dish. You can vary it with herbs—parsley, marjoram, dill, thyme, basil, orégano, sesame seeds, rosemary, tarragon, chervil. The list is endless. A work saver, pasta is an ideal substitute for potatoes.

The range of sauces that go with pasta is just as broad. There are combinations in this section. You will find many more in Kay Skinner's Buffet Favorites and in the chapter on sauces.

Experiment with herbs and sauces. You will be delighted with your new creations.

SPAGHETTI "SNACK-A-RONI"

8 ounces spaghetti
   Hot salad oil for deep
     frying

Onion salt and dillweed

Break spaghetti strands in half. Cook spaghetti as directed on package. Drain in colander. Rinse with cold water; drain again. Separate pieces of spaghetti that may cling together and drop a few at a time into oil heated to 375°. Deep fry just enough at one time to cover bottom of fry basket or fryer. Fry about 3 minutes, or until evenly and lightly browned. If necessary, separate spaghetti pieces while frying. Spread on absorbent paper to drain. Sprinkle with onion salt and dillweed. Serve with cold beverages. Makes about 4 quarts.

WARNING: When you think you've made enough, make that much more. The appealing shapes, delightful crunch and tangy flavor are reasons why this unusual snack food will disappear quickly. If there's any left over, store in a tightly covered container.

NOODLE PARTY PANCAKES

8 ounces (4 cups) fine egg noodles	¾ teaspoon salt
	¼ cup butter, melted
2 eggs	Butter for frying

Cook noodles as directed on package. Drain. Beat eggs and salt in large bowl; stir in melted butter. Add warm noodles and toss until mixed. Melt about 3 tablespoons butter in skillet over medium heat; drop tablespoons of noodle mixture into the skillet to make small pancakes. Sauté on both sides until golden brown; add more butter to skillet as needed. Serve hot with sour cream and caviar. Makes about 80.

NOTE: This same mixture can be used for larger pancakes about 3½ inches in diameter. Good with ham or bacon, served with honey or maple syrup for breakfast or lunch. Makes about 20 pancakes, 4 to 6 servings.

SPAGHETTI SQUARES

8 ounces spaghetti	¼ teaspoon garlic powder
3 eggs, beaten	¼ teaspoon white pepper
1 cup sour cream	½ cup sliced stuffed olives
½ teaspoon salt	¼ cup chopped onion
¼ teaspoon paprika	6 tablespoons butter, melted

Cook spaghetti as directed on package. Drain. In a large mixing bowl, combine spaghetti with remaining ingredients. Pour mixture into buttered 9-inch-square pan. Set in a pan of hot water; bake in 350° oven 1 hour. Cut into 1½-inch squares and fry in fat heated to 375° in deep fryer until golden brown. Drain on absorbent paper and serve warm. (These squares are also good served hot, but without being fried.) Makes 36 squares.

NOTE: This recipe can be prepared as much as a day ahead and refrigerated uncut. To serve, cut and allow to come to room temperature before frying. This also makes an excellent mealtime accompaniment to fish or chicken. Cut into larger, equal squares for 4 or 6 servings. Serve hot with your favorite cheese or tomato sauce.

DIPSY NOODLES

8 ounces (4 cups) wide egg noodles	Garlic salt or onion salt
Hot salad oil for deep frying	

Cook noodles as directed on package. Drain. Cool. Separate any noodles that may cling together, and place on absorbent paper to drain thoroughly. Cut into 2½-inch pieces. Drop a few noodles at a time into fat heated to 375°. Deep fry just enough at one time to cover bottom of fry basket or fryer. Fry about 3 minutes, or until evenly and lightly browned. If necessary, separate noodles while frying. Drain on paper towels. Sprinkle with garlic salt or onion salt. Serve with guacamole or as accompaniment to beverages and soups. Makes about 2½ quarts.

GUACAMOLE

2 very ripe large avocados
2 ripe medium tomatoes,
   peeled, seeded and
   coarsely chopped
½ cup finely chopped
   onion

1 4-ounce can green chilies
   drained and chopped
3 tablespoons lime juice
1½ teaspoons salt

Mash peeled avocados with fork, but not too smooth; the mixture should measure about 3 cups. Blend avocado with remaining ingredients; cover tightly with foil and refrigerate until serving time. Serve with Dipsy Noodles. Makes about 1 quart.

SEASHELL APPETIZERS

4 ounces (2 cups) seashell
   macaroni
¼ cup Italian salad dressing
1 cup grated Cheddar
   cheese

¼ cup minced dill pickles
2 tablespoons
   Worcestershire
⅓ cup chopped almonds
6 stuffed olives, sliced

Cook shells as directed on package. Drain. Marinate in Italian salad dressing. Blend cheese with pickles, Worcestershire and almonds. Drain shells of marinade and fill with cheese mixture. Garnish top of cheese filling with slices of olives. Insert food picks at an angle through macaroni and filling to serve. Makes about 24 appetizers.

SPAGHETTI WITH FRESH TOMATO SAUCE

12 ounces spaghetti
¼ pound bacon, diced
1 medium onion, chopped

1½ pounds tomatoes, peeled
   and diced
⅓ cup chicken bouillon

1¼ teaspoons salt
½ teaspoon basil
¼ teaspoon pepper

Freshly grated Parmesan
cheese

In a large skillet, fry bacon 2 minutes; add onion and sauté until bacon and onion are lightly browned. Mix in tomatoes, chicken bouillon, salt, basil and pepper. Simmer covered 20 minutes, stirring occasionally.

Meanwhile, cook spaghetti as directed on package. Drain. Serve with tomato sauce and cheese. Serves 4 to 6.

CASEY'S SPAGHETTI WITH CAULIFLOWER

1 pound spaghetti
1 medium head cauliflower
3 quarts water
2 teaspoons salt

¼ cup olive oil
Salt and pepper
Grated Parmesan cheese

Wash cauliflower and separate into flowerets. Cook with the water and salt in a saucepan until almost tender. Drain off 2 quarts cauliflower water, bring to a boil, and in it cook spaghetti *al dente*. Drain. Drain cauliflower and combine with spaghetti, oil and salt and pepper to taste. Arrange in serving dish and sprinkle with cheese. Serves 4 to 6.

SPAGHETTI PARMESAN

1 pound spaghetti
3 large garlic cloves,
   minced

½ cup olive oil
Freshly grated Parmesan
cheese

Sauté garlic in oil 10 minutes; do not brown. Cover and kept hot. Meanwhile, cook spaghetti as directed on package. Drain, reserving ¼ cup spaghetti water. Stir reserved spaghetti water into garlic-oil mixture. Pour over spaghetti; toss. Serve with Parmesan cheese and pass the pepper mill. Serves 8.

MACARONI SPINACH TORTINE

5¼ ounces (1¼ cups) elbow
    macaroni
    Butter
    Fine dry bread crumbs
½ cup water
1 10-ounce package frozen
    leaf spinach

4 eggs
¼ teaspoon salt
    Dash of pepper
8 ounces ricotta cheese
1 cup grated Parmesan
    cheese

Butter bottom and sides of a 9-inch-square pan; add some fine dry bread crumbs and shake pan until coated. Set pan aside. Cook macaroni as directed on package. Drain. Macaroni should measure 3 cups. Bring water to a boil in medium saucepan; add spinach and break up with a fork. Bring spinach to a boil; simmer uncovered about 2 minutes. Drain off water from saucepan and press spinach between absorbent paper to remove excess moisture. Chop spinach very fine. Beat 3 eggs with the salt and pepper thoroughly in large mixing bowl; stir in ricotta and Parmesan cheeses, spinach and 3 cups cooked macaroni. Turn mixture into prepared pan; smooth surface with spatula. Beat remaining egg in small bowl; brush on top of mixture with pastry brush. Bake in 350° oven 30 to 35 minutes, or until a metal knife inserted in center comes out clean. Run a small spatula around the sides of pan to loosen; cut into 36 squares, 1½ inches, as appetizer, or into larger squares for mealtime accompaniment. Makes 36 as appetizer or 6 as side dish. Excellent with ham or tongue. Serve warm.

NOTE: This recipe can be prepared as much as a day ahead and refrigerated uncut. To serve, allow to come to room temperature and heat in foil in 350° oven 5 to 10 minutes before cutting.

NOODLE ONION PIE

Also highly interesting for buffet meals.

Crust:

1 cup grated Cheddar cheese	¼ teaspoon dry mustard
¾ cup sifted flour	¼ cup melted butter
½ teaspoon salt	

Combine all ingredients in a bowl and mix with pastry blender or fork until smooth. Knead about 1 minute to soften. Line a 9-inch pie plate with the cheese mixture, pressing firmly to bottom and sides and fluting around rim.

Filling:

3 ounces (1½ cups) medium egg noodles	1 cup milk, scalded
	½ teaspoon salt
2 cups thinly sliced onions	¼ teaspoon pepper
2 tablespoons butter	1 cup grated Cheddar cheese
2 eggs	

Cook noodles as directed on package. Drain. Meanwhile, sauté onions in butter until tender, but not brown. Remove from heat, add noodles and toss lightly. Place in uncooked crust (above). Beat eggs slightly, and slowly stir in milk, then salt, pepper and cheese. Pour mixture over noodles. Bake in 325° oven 30-35 minutes, or until knife inserted in center comes out clean. Cut into pieces and serve as an appetizer or side dish. Serves 6 to 8 when used as a side dish. If used as an appetizer, cut into smaller pieces.

SALADS

Combining so beautifully with so many other good foods, pasta cooked and chilled is a natural salad ingredient.

Although most of these appetizing pasta salads are satisfying enough to play the role of featured attraction, a few recipes in this section are intended as accompaniments to meat, poultry or seafood dishes.

BY-THE-SEASIDE SALAD

8 ounces (2 cups) shell
   macaroni or 8 ounces
   (2 cups) elbow macaroni
3 cups diced cooked
   lobster *
1 cup sliced celery
1 cup diced cucumber
½ cup mayonnaise

3 tablespoons lemon juice
2 tablespoons capers
1 teaspoon salt
¼ teaspoon dry mustard
¼ teaspoon Tabasco
½ cup sour cream
Chicory leaves

Cook macaroni as directed on package. Drain. Cool. Combine with lobster, celery, cucumber, mayonnaise, lemon juice, capers, salt, mustard and Tabasco. Chill until serv-

   * You can use lobster tails, shrimp, crab meat, Alaskan king crab, or any combination of seafood.

ing time. Stir in sour cream; serve on crisp chicory or other salad greens. Garnish with tomato wedges if desired. Serves 4 to 6. (Recipe illustrated in color section.)

MACARONI AND TUNA GARDEN SALAD

1 pound (4 cups) elbow macaroni	1 tablespoon lemon juice
	½ teaspoon salt
2 6½- or 7-ounce cans tuna, drained	⅛ teaspoon Tabasco
	¾ cup mayonnaise
1½ cups chopped celery	½ cup sour cream
½ cup sliced stuffed olives	Crisp lettuce
2 tablespoons minced onion	1 medium tomato
	Watercress

Cook macaroni as directed on package. Drain. Cool. Combine macaroni with all ingredients except lettuce, tomato and watercress; toss lightly. Chill. Arrange on lettuce; garnish with tomato wedges and watercress. Serve with additional mayonnaise. Serves 8.

BEST-EVER SHRIMP SALAD

8 ounces (2 cups) elbow macaroni	½ teaspoon dry mustard
	½ teaspoon salt
1 cup diced celery	Dash of marjoram
1 6½-ounce can shrimps, drained and rinsed	2 tablespoons minced onion
1 cup sour cream	1 medium tomato, cut in wedges
¼ cup chili sauce	Salad greens
2 tablespoons prepared horseradish	

Cook macaroni as directed on package. Drain. Cool. Add celery and shrimps. Mix remaining ingredients thoroughly. Mix gently into macaroni mixture. Add tomato wedges. Chill. Serve on crisp greens. Serves 6. (This dish illustrated in color section.)

SHRIMP MACARONI MOUSSE

4 ounces (1 cup) elbow macaroni	¼ teaspoon salt
1 envelope unflavored gelatin	¼ teaspoon Tabasco
¼ cup cold water	2 cups chopped cooked shrimps
1¼ cups boiling water	⅔ cup sliced olives
¼ cup lemon juice	⅔ cup heavy cream
2 tablespoons sugar	Crisp greens

Cook macaroni as directed on package. Drain. Cool. Soften gelatin in cold water in a large bowl. Add boiling water and stir until completely dissolved. Stir in lemon juice, sugar, salt and Tabasco. Chill until partially set. Mix macaroni into chilled gelatin with shrimps and olives. Whip cream. Fold into macaroni mixture and turn into 1½-quart mold. Chill till firm. Unmold onto greens. Serves 8.

TUNA SUPPER SALAD

8 ounces (2 cups) elbow macaroni	¼ cup chopped sweet pickle
2 7-ounce cans tuna, drained and flaked	1 cup sour cream
1 1-pound can sliced peaches, drained	½ teaspoon salt
½ cup chopped nuts	¼ teaspoon crushed dried mint
	Dash of thyme

Cook macaroni as directed on package. Drain. Cool. Add tuna, peaches, nuts and pickle. Combine sour cream, salt, mint and thyme. Pour over tuna mixture and toss very lightly. Chill. Serves 4 to 6.

SALMON SHELL SALAD

2½ cups shell macaroni	½ cup mayonnaise
1 7¾-ounce can salmon, chilled	1 tablespoon lemon juice

1 tablespoon liquid from
salmon
½ teaspoon prepared
horseradish
1 tablespoon prepared
mustard
¼ teaspoon salt

½ cup chopped celery
½ cup chopped cucumber
1 cup cooked and seasoned
peas (optional), chilled
3 cups shredded salad
greens

Cook macaroni as directed on package. Drain. Cool. Drain
salmon and flake. Blend mayonnaise, lemon juice, liquid
from salmon, horseradish, mustard and salt. Stir flaked
salmon into mayonnaise mixture. Add celery, cucumber
and peas. Toss with macaroni, then with salad greens.
Serves 4 to 6.

SHELL-CHICKEN SALAD

8 ounces (2 cups) large
shell macaroni
½ cup mayonnaise
2 teaspoons prepared
mustard
2 tablespoons minced onion
2 cups sliced celery

⅓ cup sweet pickle relish
½ cup chopped green
pepper
½ cup whole stuffed olives
1 cup (or more) diced cooked
chicken
Lettuce

Cook macaroni as directed on package. Drain. Cool. Blend
mayonnaise with mustard until smooth. Combine with
macaroni and all remaining ingredients. Toss until well
coated with dressing. Serve on a bed of lettuce. Garnish
with pimiento strips and paprika, if desired. Serves 6 to 8.

FALL MACARONI SALAD

4 cups elbow macaroni
1 cup grated carrots
1 medium onion, chopped
1 cup chopped celery
2 1-pound cans peas, chilled
and drained

2 12-ounce cans luncheon
meat, cut in 1-inch cubes
1 cup Italian-style salad
dressing
Crisp lettuce

Cook macaroni as directed on package. Drain. Cool. Combine with carrots, onion, celery, peas, luncheon meat and salad dressing. Toss lightly, but thoroughly. Chill well before serving. Arrange on lettuce leaves. Serves 10. (This dish illustrated in color section.)

HAM, EGG AND RIGATONI SALAD

2 cups rigatoni
2 cups diced cooked ham
4 hard-cooked eggs, diced
¼ cup chopped celery
¼ cup chopped ripe olives
½ cup French dressing
Salt and pepper
Lettuce

Cook rigatoni as directed on package. Drain. Cool. Combine with remaining ingredients and mix well. Chill. Serve on crisp lettuce. Serves 4.

PICNIC MACARONI SALAD

8 ounces (2 cups) elbow macaroni
1 12-ounce can luncheon meat, cubed
1 cup sweet mixed pickles, drained
1 cup chopped celery
½ cup chopped onion
2 pimientos, chopped
2 tablespoons sweet pickle liquid
½ cup mayonnaise
1 tablespoon prepared mustard

Cook macaroni as directed on package. Drain. Cool. Combine macaroni and remaining ingredients. Toss lightly. Chill. Serves 6.

ALL SEASONS MACARONI SALAD

2 cups twirls or elbow macaroni
1 tablespoon chopped green onion
½ cup sliced radishes
1 cup sliced celery
½ cup mayonnaise
1½ tablespoons spicy brown mustard
1½ teaspoons prepared horseradish
1 teaspoon salt
Dash of white pepper

Cook twirls as directed on package. Drain. Cool. In a large bowl combine macaroni, onion, radishes and celery. Blend together mayonnaise, mustard, horseradish, salt and pepper. Toss dressing with macaroni mixture. Chill. Serves 6.

DILLED SHELL SALAD

2 cups large shell macaroni
¼ cup mayonnaise
1 teaspoon chopped chives
1 teaspoon dillweed

1 teaspoon salt
Dash of freshly ground
  pepper
12 thin slices bologna

Cook macaroni as directed on package. Drain. Cool. Combine with mayonnaise, chives, dill, salt and pepper. Toss lightly. Chill. Garnish with bologna. Serves 4 to 6.

NORWEGIAN MACARONI SALAD

8 ounces (2 cups) elbow
  macaroni
2 cups sliced cucumbers
1 cup sliced onions
½ cup vinegar
3 tablespoons water

¼ cup sugar
Salt and pepper
1 cup sour cream
1 3¾-ounce can sardines,
  drained

Cook macaroni as directed on package. Drain. Cool. Combine cucumbers, onions, vinegar, water, sugar, and salt and pepper to taste. Chill 1 hour; drain. Combine cucumber mixture, macaroni, sour cream and sardines. Toss lightly. Chill. Serves 4 to 6.

RANCHO MACARONI SALAD

8 ounces (2 cups) elbow
  macaroni
1 15-ounce can red kidney
  beans, drained
1 cup sour cream

⅓ cup chopped celery
1 cup drained sweet mixed
  pickles, coarsely
  chopped

¼ cup sweet pickle liquid
2 tablespoons lemon juice
1 teaspoon salt
1 teaspoon dried chives
½ teaspoon onion salt
Pepper

2 to 3 teaspoons prepared
horseradish
½ pound sliced salami, cut
into thin strips
Crisp salad greens

Cook macaroni as directed on package. Drain. Cool. Combine macaroni, kidney beans, sour cream, celery, pickles, pickle liquid, lemon juice and remaining seasonings; toss and chill. Add salami and toss before serving on salad greens. Serves 4 to 6.

MACARONI FRUIT SALAD

8 ounces (1½ cups) salad
macaroni
1 cup sour cream
1 cup creamed cottage
cheese
2 tablespoons chopped
pecans
½ teaspoon salt
¼ teaspoon cinnamon

1 cup drained orange
sections
1 20½-ounce can pineapple
chunks, drained
3 tablespoons pineapple
syrup
Salad greens
1 26-ounce can apricot
halves, drained

Cook macaroni as directed on package. Drain. Cool. Mix together macaroni, sour cream, cottage cheese, pecans, salt and cinnamon. Add orange sections, pineapple and 3 tablespoons of the pineapple syrup. Toss lightly and chill. Mound on salad greens; surround with apricots. Garnish with cinnamon and serve with additional sour cream if desired. Serves 6.

MACARONI SUPPER SALAD PLATTER

8 ounces (2 cups) elbow
macaroni
½ cup olive or salad oil
¼ cup vinegar

1 tablespoon prepared
mustard
1 teaspoon chopped chives
Salt

¼ cup chopped canned
   pimientos
6 deviled egg halves
½ pound thinly sliced ham,
   rolled

2 tomatoes, quartered
Lettuce
Parsley

Cook macaroni according to package directions. Drain.
Combine oil, vinegar, mustard, chives, and salt to taste;
blend or shake well. Add with pimientos to macaroni;
toss well. Chill. Arrange macaroni mixture, deviled eggs,
ham rolls and tomatoes on lettuce. Garnish with parsley.
Serves 6. (This dish illustrated in color section.)

GOURMET DISHES

One of the greatest gourmet pasta dishes of all time was concocted by Rossini, composer of the opera *William Tell*. Rossini's macaroni, first softened and swollen by the gentle caress of slowly boiling water, was dried on a fresh linen cloth. It was then stuffed with a rich mixture of chicken livers, tender truffles, a few glasses of old Malvoisie, and a small amount of orange juice and nutmeg. Then it was placed in a silver casserole and baked, while savory vapors permeated the air. It is said that Rossini claimed that this dish merited as great fame as his music. (Sorry, but the actual recipe is lost to time.)

Gourmet cooking is often thought of as time consuming, though this is not necessarily the case. Some of the recipes in this chapter take quite a lot of preparation, others are simple and fairly quick. Several are of foreign origin.

There are also a few dessert recipes to intrigue you.

SPAGHETTI BOLOGNESE

1 pound spaghetti	1 cup finely chopped onion
1 cup thinly sliced celery	1 cup shredded carrot

Pasta recipes are quick and easy to make. Often neglected are the possibilities in a cold dish like this simple but elegant By-the-Seaside Salad (page 84), adaptable to shrimp, crab or any combination of seafood as well as lobster.

A Mediterranean favorite, Macaroni with Greek-Style Stew
(page 102) combines lamb or beef with eggplant and okra.

Great party dishes: Noodles Alfredo (above, page 58) in a chafing dish, and Sunday Supper Ring (below, page 65), molded noodles with a cheese sauce and Brussels sprouts.

Easy combinations with pasta are, top to bottom, Tomato Noodle Soup (not requiring any recipe), Fall Macaroni Salad (page 87) and Spaghetti with Meat Sauce (page 33).

Ideal for macaroni supper menus, three all-American favorites: Macaroni Supper Salad Platter (top, page 90), Spaghetti and Chicken Skillet (left, page 56), and Best-Ever Shrimp Salad (right, page 85).

As exotic to serve as it is delicious to eat, Macaroni
Oriental (page 104) combines thinly sliced sautéed beef
or pork with onions, celery, spinach and water chestnuts.

2 tablespoons olive oil
1 tablespoon butter
2 pounds ground beef
   chuck
¼ pound bulk sausage
   meat
2 small bay leaves
1½ teaspoons salt
⅛ teaspoon freshly grated
   nutmeg

¼ teaspoon pepper
1 cup Chianti (dry red
   wine)
1 28-ounce can plum
   tomatoes
1 6-ounce can tomato
   paste
Wedge of Parmesan
   cheese

In a large saucepan, sauté celery, onion and carrot in oil and butter until crisp-tender. Remove with slotted spoon. In same skillet, brown chuck and sausage; drain off excess fat, if necessary. Return vegetables to meat; add seasonings, wine, tomatoes and tomato paste. Simmer covered 1 hour; uncover and simmer 1 hour longer, stirring occasionally.

Cook spaghetti as directed on package. Drain. Serve with sauce. Parmesan cheese should be individually grated at table and sprinkled on to taste. Serves 8.

SPAGHETTI WITH VEGETABLE SAUCE

1 pound spaghetti
1 medium eggplant, peeled
   and cut in 3-inch strips,
   ½ inch thick
2 medium zucchini, cut in
   ½-inch slices
½ cup olive oil
2 medium yellow onions,
   thinly sliced
2 medium green peppers,
   thinly sliced

2 garlic cloves, minced
5 medium firm tomatoes,
   peeled and cut in slices
2 teaspoons salt
½ teaspoon coarsely ground
   black pepper
½ teaspoon basil
½ teaspoon orégano
1 tablespoon capers
¼ cup chopped parsley

In a Dutch oven, sauté eggplant strips, then zucchini slices, in ¼ cup hot oil 1 minute on each side; remove. In same pan, cook onions, green peppers and garlic in remaining oil until tender. Place tomato slices on top; cook covered 5 minutes. Gently stir in eggplant, zucchini, salt, and remaining ingredients except spaghetti. Simmer covered 25 minutes.

Meanwhile, cook spaghetti as directed on package. Drain. Serve sauce over spaghetti with freshly grated Permesan cheese if desired. Serves 6 to 8.

MACARONI PASTITSIO
(A Greek dish)

1 pound (4 cups) elbow
    macaroni
1 cup chopped onions
2 tablespoons butter
2 pounds ground beef
    chuck
1 10½-ounce can tomato
    purée
1 6-ounce can tomato
    paste

2 teaspoons salt
¼ teaspoon pepper
¼ teaspoon cinnamon
⅓ cup fine dry bread
    crumbs
1 egg
    Rich White Sauce (below)
1½ cups grated Parmesan
    cheese

Cook macaroni as directed on package. Drain. Cool to lukewarm. In a large skillet, sauté onions in butter until golden. Add beef and brown evenly. Stir in tomato purée, tomato paste, salt, pepper and cinnamon. Simmer, covered, 30 minutes. Add bread crumbs. Beat egg in a large kettle, add macaroni and toss. In a large rectangular baking pan (13x9x2 inches), arrange in layers half of macaroni, the meat mixture, remaining macaroni and then rich white sauce on top, sprinkling each layer with Parmesan cheese. Bake in 375° oven 30 minutes, or until cheese browns lightly. Let stand 10 minutes, then cut into square portions. Serves 8 to 10.

Rich White Sauce: Melt ⅓ cup butter in saucepan; blend in ⅓ cup flour, 1½ teaspoons salt, ¼ teaspoon pepper and ⅛ teaspoon nutmeg. Gradually add 2½ cups milk; cook, stirring constantly, until sauce boils 1 minute. Blend ½ cup milk and 2 eggs; stir into sauce. Cook and stir over medium heat until sauce thickens.

NOTE: *For future use:* Cool macaroni, meat filling and sauce quickly. Line baking pan with heavy-duty foil, allowing extra foil for fold. Layer ingredients in pan. Seal with double fold. Freeze; remove from pan. When ready to use, remove foil; replace Pastitsio in buttered baking pan. Cover; bake unthawed in 375° oven 1½ hours. Uncover and bake 45 minutes longer, or until hot.

Alternate method for future use: Omit the egg and do not prepare the rich white sauce. Proceed as in the method above. For serving, allow Pastitsio to defrost in refrigerator overnight. Bake covered in 375° oven 15 minutes. Meanwhile, prepare the rich white sauce. Pour over Pastitsio and bake uncovered 30 minutes.

CLASSIC LASAGNE

1 pound lasagne
1 medium onion, chopped
2 garlic cloves, crushed
4 tablespoons olive oil
1 28-ounce can tomatoes
2 6-ounce cans tomato paste
½ cup water
1 teaspoon salt
½ teaspoon orégano
½ teaspoon basil
⅛ teaspoon crushed red pepper

1 pound ground beef chuck
½ pound ground lean pork
¼ cup chopped parsley
2 eggs
½ cup fine dry bread crumbs
Freshly grated Parmesan cheese (about ½ cup)
⅛ teaspoon black pepper
1 pound ricotta or creamed cottage cheese
½ pound mozzarella cheese, sliced

In a saucepan, sauté onion and garlic in 2 tablespoons of the oil until lightly browned. Add tomatoes, tomato paste, water, ½ teaspoon salt, the herbs and red pepper. Simmer, covered, 1 hour.

Mix together beef, pork, parsley, eggs, bread crumbs, 2 tablespoons Parmesan cheese, black pepper and ½ teaspoon salt. Shape into ½-inch meat balls. Sauté in remaining 2 tablespoons oil until browned; add to sauce and simmer 15 minutes.

Cook lasagne as directed on package. Drain. Layer in a large pan (13x9x2¼ inches): sauce with meat balls, lasagne, dollops of ricotta and Parmesan cheese. Repeat layers until all ingredients are used; top with mozzarella slices. Bake in 375° oven 25 minutes.

VARIATION: To make lasagne with meat sauce instead of meat balls, proceed as above, except brown meat with onion and garlic. Omit remaining 2 tablespoons oil, eggs, bread crumbs and black pepper. Add 1 teaspoon salt, ¼ teaspoon red pepper and remaining sauce ingredients; simmer covered 1 hour. Complete dish by layering as above.

LASAGNE ROLLS WITH MEAT SAUCE

1 pound lasagne	4 6-ounce cans tomato
1 pound sweet Italian	paste
sausage, sliced	1 cup water
2 pounds ground beef	1 tablespoon salt
chuck	2 teaspoons Italian
2 medium onions, chopped	seasoning
4 garlic cloves, minced	¼ teaspoon pepper
2 28-ounce cans plum	Cheese Filling (see next
tomatoes	page)

Brown sausage in heavy saucepan, then remove sausage. In same pan brown beef, stirring frequently. Return sausage. Add onions, garlic, tomatoes, tomato paste, water, salt, Italian seasoning and pepper. Simmer covered 1 hour. Cook lasagne as directed on package. Drain. Lay noodles on absorbent or waxed paper. Spread about ¼ cup of cheese filling on each lasagne noodle. Fold each noodle over 1 inch and continue folding, making a roll. Pour about 3 cups of the prepared meat sauce in each of two large baking pans (13x9x2 inches). Place lasagne rolls seam side down in pans. Pour remaining meat sauce over lasagne. Bake uncovered in 350° oven 35 minutes. Serve with grated Parmesan cheese. Serves 8.

Cheese Filling: Whip 2 pounds ricotta cheese. Add 1 teaspoon salt, ¼ teaspoon pepper, ¼ teaspoon nutmeg, ¼ pound shredded mozzarella cheese, ¼ cup grated Parmesan cheese and ¼ cup finely chopped parsley; mix well. Makes about 4 cups.

CREAMY LASAGNE

8 ounces lasagne
1 pound pork sausage links, parboiled 1 minute
½ pound ground beef (optional)
2 garlic cloves, minced
½ teaspoon salt

Rich Cream Sauce (below)
1 pound ricotta or creamed cottage cheese
1 cup grated Parmesan cheese
½ pound mozzarella cheese, sliced

Thinly slice sausage and combine with beef, garlic and salt in large skillet. Brown thoroughly over high heat, stirring frequently; set aside. Cook lasagne as directed on package. Drain. In bottom of a large baking pan (13x9x2 inches), pour a small amount of rich cream sauce. Layer half of lasagne, meat, ricotta, Parmesan and sauce. Repeat layers. Top with mozzarella cheese. Bake in 375° oven 20 minutes. Broil 4 inches from source of heat 1 to 2 minutes, or until browned. Serves 8.

Rich Cream Sauce:

Chop 1 medium onion and sauté in 3 tablespoons butter until crisp-tender. Stir in 3 tablespoons flour, 1½ teaspoons salt, ¼ teaspoon pepper and ¼ teaspoon nutmeg.

Gradually add 1 cup milk and 1 cup light cream; cook over medium heat, stirring constantly until sauce thickens. Blend 1 cup light cream and 2 egg yolks; stir into sauce. Cook and stir 1 minute longer. Makes 3 cups.

RIGATONI MILANESE

4 cups rigatoni	2 eggs
½ pound ground beef chuck	½ teaspoon garlic powder
¼ pound ground fresh pork	1½ teaspoons salt
¾ cup fine dry bread crumbs	Dash of pepper
1 cup grated Parmesan cheese	1 tablespoon minced parsley
	Italian Rigatoni Sauce (below)

Cook rigatoni as directed on package. Drain. Rinse quickly with cold water so you can handle the pasta. Combine beef, pork, bread crumbs, ½ cup of the cheese, eggs, garlic powder, salt, pepper and parsley; mix throughly. Stuff rigatoni with the mixture. Arrange a single layer of the stuffed pasta on bottom of 3-quart baking dish. Top with some of the sauce. Continue layering in this manner until all is used. Sprinkle with remaining ½ cup Parmesan, cover, and bake in 350° oven 1 hour. Uncover, and bake 15 minutes longer. Serves 6.

ITALIAN RIGATONI SAUCE

½ pound ground beef	2 teaspoons salt
⅔ cup chopped onion	¼ teaspoon pepper
3 tablespoons olive oil	1 6-ounce can tomato paste plus 1 can water
1 teaspoon orégano	
1 medium bay leaf	1 28-ounce can tomatoes

Sauté ground beef and onion in the oil about 5 minutes, or until just lightly browned. Add remaining ingredients and simmer for about 10 minutes.

STUFFED BEEF ROLL WITH SAFFRON NOODLES

8 ounces (4 cups) medium egg noodles	2 tablespoons dry bread crumbs
½ cup chopped celery	¼ teaspoon salt
⅓ cup chopped green pepper	¼ teaspoon pepper
¼ cup chopped onion	¼ teaspoon garlic salt
1 tablespoon butter	1 egg, slightly beaten
1 3-ounce can chopped broiled mushrooms	1 pimiento, cut in strips
1½ pounds ground beef round	¼ teaspoon saffron
2 tablespoons grated Parmesan cheese	Brown Mushroom Gravy (below) (optional)

Cook celery, green pepper and onion in butter 3 minutes. Drain mushrooms; reserve liquid for gravy. Add mushrooms to vegetables; set aside. Mix together beef, cheese, bread crumbs, salt, pepper, garlic salt and egg; blend well. On plastic film, pat meat mixture into ½-inch layer 10x8 inches. Spoon vegetables lengthwise across center; add pimiento strips. With the aid of the plastic film roll meat mixture over filling into a roll 8x3½x2½ inches. Place "seam" side down and chill about 1 hour. Bake in lightly buttered shallow baking pan in 375° oven 1 hour.

Meanwhile cook noodles as directed on package, adding saffron to water. Drain. Serve sliced meat roll on noodles with brown mushroom gravy, if desired. Serves 6.

Brown Mushroom Gravy:

Remove excess fat from roasting pan; stir reserved mushroom liquid into pan drippings. Pour into measuring cup; add liquid from additional 3-ounce can of chopped broiled mushrooms. Add water to measure 1½ cups; gradually stir about ¼ cup of the liquid into 1 tablespoon flour to form a smooth paste. Add remaining liquid and mushrooms. Bring to a boil, stirring constantly; boil 1 minute. Season to taste. Makes 1⅔ cups.

STUFFED VEAL SCALLOPS PARMESAN

8 ounces (2 cups) elbow macaroni	1 teaspoon salt
4 slices bacon	1 teaspoon rosemary
½ cup grated Parmesan cheese	¼ teaspoon pepper
⅓ cup minced parsley	1 pound very thin veal scallops
½ cup flour	2 cups water

Fry bacon until crisp; reserve bacon drippings. Drain bacon on absorbent paper. Crumble. Cook macaroni as directed on package. Drain. Mix with bacon, ¼ cup of the cheese and ¼ cup of the parsley. Combine flour, salt, rosemary and pepper on waxed paper. Dredge veal scallops with mixture, shake off excess, and reserve. Place rounded tablespoons of macaroni mixture in center of each scallop, roll up veal around filling, and secure with food picks or skewers. Brown in hot bacon fat.

Place remaining macaroni mixture in lightly buttered 2-quart casserole. Arrange scallops on top. Stir reserved flour mixture into meat drippings in skillet. Add water and cook, stirring constantly, until mixture thickens. Pour over veal and macaroni in casserole. Sprinkle with remaining cheese and cover. Bake in 350° oven 40 minutes, or until meat is tender. Uncover, sprinkle with remaining parsley, and serve at once. Serves 4.

DUMPLINGS WITH PROSCIUTTO

4 cups dumplings	½ cup grated Parmesan cheese
¼ cup butter	
¼ pound prosciutto, diced	½ teaspoon salt
½ cup boiling water	Freshly ground pepper

Melt butter, add prosciutto and brown lightly. Add water and simmer 5 minutes. Meanwhile, cook dumplings as directed on package. Drain. Pour prosciutto sauce over. Add cheese, salt and pepper and toss well to mix. Serves 2 as an entrée, 4 as a first course.

BAMI
(An Indonesian dish)

4 ounces vermicelli
1 small head very young cabbage, chopped
2 green onions, thinly sliced
2 celery ribs, chopped

1 garlic clove, mashed
3 tablespoons butter
1 cup slivered cooked pork
1 pound shrimps, cooked and peeled

Cook vermicelli as directed on package. Drain. Meanwhile, fry cabbage, onions, celery and garlic in butter for 10 minutes, stirring constantly. Add pork and shrimps and heat through. Serve over the vermicelli. Serves 4.

CHICKEN AND NOODLES IN WINE SAUCE

8 ounces (4 cups) medium egg noodles
2 broiler-fryers, quartered
Flour
½ cup butter
½ cup finely chopped onion
1 garlic clove, crushed
¼ teaspoon rosemary
¼ teaspoon marjoram
½ cup flour

4 cups chicken broth
1½ cups tomatoes, peeled, quartered
2 teaspoons salt
½ teaspoon pepper
1 small bay leaf
1 small carrot
3 celery ribs
½ pound fresh mushrooms, sliced
½ cup white wine

Wipe chicken pieces and dredge with flour. Sauté in butter until golden. Remove chicken from pan. Add onion and sauté until soft. Add garlic, rosemary and marjoram and cook a few minutes longer, but do not brown. Blend in ½ cup flour. Gradually add chicken broth and cook, stirring constantly, until thickened. Add tomatoes, salt, pepper, chicken, bay leaf, carrot and celery ribs. Simmer slowly 15 minutes. Add mushrooms and wine. Bring to a boil. Cover, reduce heat, and simmer slowly 30 minutes, or until chicken is tender. Remove bay leaf, carrot and celery.

Meanwhile, cook noodles as directed on package. Drain. Place on a heated serving dish. Top with chicken and pour sauce over all. Serves 4 to 6.

JAPANESE CHICKEN IN THE POT

8 ounces (4 cups) fine egg
    noodles
2 quarts chicken stock
2 cooked broiler-fryers, cut
    into serving pieces

8 mushrooms
8 leaves of Chinese
    cabbage, rolled up
Salt and pepper

Put stock and chicken pieces into a pot and allow to simmer 5 minutes. Add mushrooms, cabbage rolls (which unroll while cooking) and noodles in the pot and boil hard until noodles are cooked, 8 to 10 minutes. Season to taste with salt and pepper. The Japanese serve the soup separately in little cups. Serving dishes are arranged with a little soy sauce, some chopped green onion and a little freshly grated horseradish in the bottom. The chicken, mushrooms and cabbage are placed on top. Each diner mixes up the contents of his own plate. Serves 4.

MACARONI WITH GREEK-STYLE STEW

8 ounces (2 cups) elbow
    macaroni

2 pounds lean cubed lamb
    or beef

2 tablespoons salad oil	1 small eggplant, cut in ½-inch thick slices
2 medium onions, sliced	
1 can (8 ounces) tomato sauce	1 large green pepper, diced
¼ cup water	½ pound okra, trimmed (or green beans, cut)
1 teaspoon salt	
½ teaspoon marjoram	2 medium tomatoes, peeled and sliced
¼ teaspoon pepper	

Cook macaroni as directed on package. Drain. Brown meat in oil in Dutch oven or large saucepan; drain off drippings. Add onions to meat; sauté about 5 minutes. Stir in tomato sauce, water, 1 teaspoon salt, the marjoram and the pepper. Simmer covered 45 minutes. Add eggplant, green pepper and okra. Simmer 30 minutes or until meat and vegetables are tender. Add tomatoes; cook uncovered 5 to 10 minutes, stirring occasionally. Serve over macaroni. Serves 4 to 6. (This recipe illustrated in color section.)

CAPRI SPAGHETTI DINNER

8 ounces spaghetti	¼ pound Cheddar cheese, sliced
2 6½-ounce cans tuna, drained	
3 cups Cheddar Cheese Sauce (below)	¼ cup sliced stuffed olives

Cook spaghetti as directed on package. Drain. Combine spaghetti with tuna and cheese sauce. Turn into a 1½-quart baking dish, and arrange cheese slices around edge. Bake in 350° oven 25 minutes. Remove and top with sliced olives. Serves 6.

Cheddar Cheese Sauce:

Melt ¼ cup butter in saucepan; blend in ¼ cup flour. Gradually stir in 2½ cups milk; continue stirring until sauce boils for 1 minute. Add 1 teaspoon dry mustard, 1 tablespoon prepared horseradish, ½ teaspoon salt and dash of white pepper; remove from heat and stir in ½ cup grated Cheddar cheese. Makes 3 cups.

MACARONI ORIENTAL

1½ pounds (6 cups) elbow macaroni

3 pounds thinly sliced beef sirloin or boned loin of pork cut in strips

½ cup butter or margarine

¾ pound fresh mushrooms, sliced

2 medium Bermuda onions, sliced

3 bunches green onions or scallions, cut in 1-inch pieces

6 cups diagonally sliced celery

3 10-ounce packages fresh spinach, torn

3 5-ounce cans water chestnuts, drained and sliced

6 beef bouillon cubes, dissolved in 3 cups hot water

3 tablespoons cornstarch

¾ cup soy sauce

¾ cup sherry (optional)

Cook macaroni as directed on package. Drain. Meanwhile, in Dutch oven or kettle, sauté beef in butter until lightly browned (when using pork sauté 5 minutes); add mushrooms and sauté 2 minutes. Add onions, celery, spinach, water chestnuts and bouillon; cook covered 3 minutes. Blend cornstarch with soy sauce. Stir into kettle and boil 1 minute. Add sherry and heat. Serve over macaroni with additional soy sauce, as desired. Serves 12. (This dish illustrated in color section.)

HAWAIIAN SHRIMPS AND MACARONI

8 ounces (2 cups) elbow macaroni

2 12-ounce packages frozen shrimps, thawed

Flour

3 tablespoons salad oil

1 20-ounce can pineapple chunks

⅓ cup vinegar

¼ cup packed brown sugar

½ teaspoon salt

1½ tablespoons soy sauce

1 tablespoon cornstarch

2 tablespoons water

1 green pepper, coarsely diced

Cook macaroni as directed on package. Drain. Meanwhile, roll shrimps in flour. Brown in hot oil in skillet; remove shrimps. Drain pineapple and add ½ cup of the syrup to skillet with vinegar, brown sugar, salt and soy sauce. Bring to a boil; mix cornstarch with water and add to skillet. Cook, stirring constantly, until clear and thickened. Add shrimps, pineapple and green pepper. Cook and stir until green pepper is almost tender. Stir in macaroni. Serves 4 to 6.

LOBSTER AND RIGATONI

4 cups rigatoni	Freshly ground pepper
2 tablespoons butter	1 5½-ounce can lobster, drained
¼ pound mushrooms, sliced	
¼ cup chopped parsley	1 cup sour cream
1 teaspoon dry mustard	½ cup grated Parmesan cheese
½ teaspoon salt	

Cook rigatoni as directed on package. Drain. Melt butter; add mushrooms and sauté 5 minutes. Add parsley, mustard, salt and pepper to taste. Break lobster into small pieces; discard bony tissue. Add with sour cream to sauce. Mix lightly and heat thoroughly. Place rigatoni in 4 to 6 buttered individual casseroles and pour sauce over each. Sprinkle with cheese. Broil 3 to 4 inches from source of heat until cheese is melted and brown. Serves 4 to 6.

NOODLES ROMANOFF

8 ounces (4 cups) fine egg noodles	1 tablespoon Worcestershire
1 cup cottage cheese	Dash of Tabasco
1 cup sour cream	Salt
1 garlic clove, minced	1 cup grated Parmesan cheese
1 onion, chopped fine	

Cook noodles as directed on package. Drain. Mix with cottage cheese, sour cream, garlic, onion, Worcestershire,

Tabasco and salt to taste; pour into buttered casserole. Bake in 350° oven until brown and crusty on top, about 45 minutes. Serve the Parmesan separately so that each guest may top his serving of noodles as he likes. Serves 6 to 8.

RIPPLET NOODLES ALLA MILANO

8 ounces (4 cups) ripplet egg noodles
⅓ pound prosciutto, cut into very thin strips
1 cup cooked peas
4 tablespoons butter
½ cup heavy cream

Cook ripplet noodles as directed on package. Drain. Return to pan, add other ingredients, and toss constantly until well heated through. Serves 2 as an entrée, 4 as a first course.

PARMA NOODLES

8 ounces (4 cups) wide egg noodles
⅔ cup and 4 tablespoons butter
¼ pound prosciutto, cut into very thin strips
¾ cup light cream
1 cup Meat-Mushroom Sauce (page 74)
1 cup grated Parmesan cheese

Melt the ⅔ cup butter. Add prosciutto and cook 1 minute. Pour in cream and meat-mushroom sauce. Simmer gently 10 minutes. Meanwhile, cook noodles as directed on package. Drain. Return to pan and pour the sauce over. Cut remaining butter into fine pieces and put with the cheese on top of noodles; toss well. Serves 4 as an entrée, 6 to 8 as a first course.

APPLE AND NOODLE DESSERT

4 ounces (2 cups) fine egg noodles
1½ cups sliced apples
1¼ cups water

¼ cup chopped nuts
¼ cup dried currants
½ teaspoon cinnamon
½ cup brown sugar

1 tablespoon lemon juice
½ teaspoon salt
1 tablespoon melted butter
Heavy cream

Arrange apple slices in buttered 1-quart casserole. Cover, and bake in 375° oven 15 minutes. Meanwhile, cook noodles as directed on package. Drain. Spread over apples. Mix remaining ingredients and pour over noodles. Return to oven and bake 15 minutes longer. Serve with plain or whipped cream. Serves 4.

CREAMY NOODLE PUDDING

4 ounces (2 cups) medium
egg noodles
2 cups scalded milk
2 eggs, beaten
½ cup sugar
½ teaspoon salt

1 teaspoon vanilla extract
1 teaspoon grated lemon
rind
½ cup seedless raisins
Nutmeg
Cream

Cook noodles as directed on package. Drain. Meanwhile, combine milk, eggs, sugar, salt, vanilla and lemon rind. Fold in raisins and noodles. Pour into buttered individual custard cups. Sprinkle with nutmeg. Set custard cups in pan of hot water. Bake in 350° oven 1 hour. Unmold into sauce dishes. Serve with cream. Serves 4.

NOODLE CONFECTION

8 ounces (4 cups) wide egg
noodles
Hot salad oil for deep
frying

Confectioners' sugar

Cook noodles as directed on package. Drain. Cool. Separate any noodles that may cling together and drop a few at a time into fat heated to 375°. Deep fry just enough at one time to cover bottom of fry basket or fryer. Fry about 3 minutes, or until evenly and lightly browned. If necessary, separate noodles while frying. Spread on absorbent paper to drain. Sprinkle or shake in paper bag with confectioners' sugar. (Or shake with mixture of cinnamon and granulated sugar.) Serve with coffee or tea, fruit or ice cream. Makes about 2½ quarts.

QUICK & EASY PASTA DISHES

Shopping days, volunteer activities, friends dropping in unexpectedly, all call for recipes that are easy to make in a minimum of time. It is a good idea to keep a few extra packages of pasta on hand for emergencies, rounding out the menu from your freezer and pantry. A hot vegetable, a tossed salad, some fruit or a packaged dessert complete the meal.

TIME-SAVER SPAGHETTI AND MEAT SAUCE

8 ounces spaghetti	¼ cup slivered ripe olives
1 pound lean ground beef	1 bay leaf
⅓ cup sliced celery	1 teaspoon basil
¼ cup sliced onion	½ teaspoon salt
1 tablespoon salad oil	
2 8-ounce cans tomato	
sauce with mushrooms	

Sauté beef, celery and onion in oil until lightly browned. Stir in tomato sauce, olives, bay leaf, basil and salt. Simmer 15 minutes. Meanwhile, cook spaghetti as directed on package. Drain. Serve with meat sauce. Serves 4.

CHILI SPAGHETTI

8 ounces spaghetti	2 tablespoons butter
1 medium onion, finely chopped	2 1-pound cans chili con carne with beans

Cook spaghetti as directed on package. Drain. Sauté onion in butter until tender. Add chili and heat to serving temperature, stirring occasionally. Serve spaghetti topped with chili mixture. Serves 4.

MACARONI CASSEROLE ITALIANO

8 ounces (2 cups) elbow macaroni	½ pound hot Italian sausage, parboiled 4 minutes and sliced
1 1½-ounce envelope spaghetti sauce mix with mushrooms	½ pound ground beef
1 6-ounce can tomato paste (with 3 cans water)	1 medium onion, chopped
	½ teaspoon salt
	Freshly grated Parmesan cheese

Blend sauce mix, tomato paste, and 3 cans water in a saucepan. In a skillet, brown sausage; add to sauce. In same skillet, brown beef with onion and salt, stirring frequently. Stir into sauce and bring to a boil. Simmer, covered, 25 to 30 minutes. Meanwhile, cook macaroni as directed on package. Drain. Combine with meat sauce in 2-quart casserole. Sprinkle cheese on top. Bake uncovered in 375° oven 20 minutes. Serves 4.

HURRY-UP MACARONI TUNA CASSEROLE

8 ounces (2 cups) elbow macaroni	1 10½-ounce can condensed cream of mushroom soup
2 6½- to 7-ounce cans tuna, drained and flaked	

¼ cup sliced stuffed olives
¾ cup milk
1 cup grated Cheddar
cheese

Tomato wedges or slices
(optional)

Cook macaroni as directed on package. Drain. Mix together macaroni, tuna, soup, olives, milk and cheese. Turn into buttered 1½-quart casserole. Garnish with tomato wedges or slices. Sprinkle with bread crumbs, if desired. Bake in 375° oven 20 minutes or until bubbly. Serves 4 to 6.

EGGS GOLDENROD

2 cups elbow macaroni
1 10½-ounce can condensed
asparagus soup
½ cup milk
¾ cup cubed Cheddar
cheese
1 tablespoon instant minced
onion

1 tablespoon parsley flakes
2 teaspoons prepared
mustard
6 stuffed olives, sliced
4 hard-cooked eggs, sliced
Toast or English muffins

Cook macaroni as directed on package. Drain. Combine soup and milk and stir over low heat until well blended. Add cheese and stir until melted. Add onion, parsley, mustard and olives and blend well. Add macaroni and egg slices and heat to piping hot. Serve over buttered toast triangles or English muffins. Serves 4.

SHELL MACARONI WITH SHRIMPS

8 ounces (2 cups) shell
macaroni
1 large onion, chopped
1 garlic clove, minced
½ cup salad oil

½ cup tomato juice
1 cup chopped parsley
1 5-ounce can shrimps,
drained and rinsed
Salt and pepper

Cook macaroni as directed on package. Drain. Meanwhile, sauté onion and garlic in oil until onion is transparent. Add tomato juice, parsley and shrimps and cook, stirring often, about 2 minutes, or until parsley is wilted. Season to taste. Toss with macaroni. Serves 4.

CHEESY SHRIMP SUPPER

1 pound Italian style spaghetti
2 tablespoons butter
1 teaspoon instant minced onion
2 teaspoons parsley flakes
2 10½-ounce cans condensed cream of celery soup

½ can milk
1 cup cooked or canned shrimps
1 cup shredded Swiss cheese or Gruyère
¼ teaspoon Tabasco

Cook spaghetti as directed on package. Drain. Mix well with butter, onion and parsley. Meanwhile, combine soup with milk and heat. Add shrimps, Tabasco, and cheese and heat to piping hot. Pour over hot spaghetti. Serves 4 or 5.

BEEF SKILLET SUPPER

2 cups large shell macaroni
2 tablespoons butter
2 teaspoons minced onion
1 pound ground beef chuck
1 teaspoon celery salt

Freshly ground pepper
1 10½-ounce can condensed cream of mushroom soup
¾ cup milk

Cook macaroni as directed on package. Drain. Heat butter and sauté onion over low heat until soft. Add beef and cook, stirring constantly, until browned. Add seasonings, soup and milk and blend well. Add macaroni and heat to piping hot. Serves 4.

QUICK SAUSAGE CASSEROLE

2 cups ready-cut spaghetti
8 sausage patties
1 10½-ounce can
   condensed tomato soup

⅓ cup milk
½ cup sliced ripe olives
   Broken corn chips

Cook spaghetti as directed on package. Drain. Place in buttered shallow 2-quart casserole. Brown patties on both sides. Combine soup and milk and blend until smooth. Add olives. Place patties on top of spaghetti and pour sauce over all. Sprinkle with corn chips. Bake in 375° oven 15 to 20 minutes. Serves 4.

SAL-MAC CASSEROLE

1 cup elbow macaroni
1 10½-ounce can
   condensed cream of
   celery soup
¾ cup hot water
1 tablespoon instant minced
   onion

2 tablespoons chopped
   pimiento
1 1-pound can salmon,
   drained and flaked
½ cup cracker crumbs
2 tablespoons butter

Cook macaroni as directed on package. Drain. Meanwhile, heat soup and water in a saucepan. Stir in onion, pimiento and salmon. Mix with drained macaroni. Place in buttered 1½-quart casserole and top with crumbs. Dot with butter. Bake in 350° oven until golden brown on top, about 20 minutes. Serves 4.

QUICK SPAGHETTI AND MEAT BALLS

12 ounces long spaghetti
1 28-ounce can tomatoes
1 1½-ounce package
   spaghetti sauce mix
   with mushrooms

1 15½-ounce can meat balls
   in gravy
   Grated Parmesan cheese

Cook spaghetti as directed on package. Drain. Meanwhile, blend tomatoes with sauce mix and bring to a boil. Add meat balls and gravy, reduce heat, and simmer until well heated. Place spaghetti on large heated platter and pour meat balls and sauce over top. Serve with plenty of grated Parmesan cheese. Serves 6.

COMPANY SEAFARING NOODLES

4 ounces (2 cups) wide egg
    noodles
¼ cup butter
¼ cup flour
½ teaspoon salt
¼ teaspoon pepper

2 cups milk
2 egg yolks, beaten
1 tablespoon sherry
2 cups cooked lobster, tuna,
    shrimps and/or crab
    meat

Melt butter over low heat. Blend in flour and seasonings. Add milk and cook, stirring constantly, until thickened. Mix some of the sauce with egg yolks. Return to sauce and blend well. Stir in sherry and seafood and heat through, but do not boil. Meanwhile, cook noodles as directed on package. Drain. Pour seafood sauce over noodles and decorate with parsley sprigs and pimiento strips, if desired. Serves 4.

SPEEDY SPAGHETTI ENTRÉE

8 ounces spaghetti
1 12-ounce can luncheon
    meat, cut in thin strips,
    or 2 cups diced cooked
    ham
2 tablespoons salad oil

2 eggs
½ cup freshly grated
    Parmesan cheese
Salt and pepper
¼ cup chopped parsley

Cook spaghetti as directed on package. Drain. Meanwhile, sauté meat in oil until lightly browned. Beat eggs with ¼ cup of the cheese; add to hot spaghetti, stirring quickly to cook the eggs. Add undrained meat and salt and pepper to taste. Mix lightly and turn into serving dish. Sprinkle parsley and remaining cheese on top. Serves 4.

CHICKEN-LICKIN'

8 ounces spaghetti	½ pound mushrooms,
¾ cup butter	chopped
½ pound chicken livers,	½ cup chopped parsley
chopped	Salt and pepper

Cook spaghetti as directed on package. Drain. Meanwhile melt butter. Add livers, mushrooms, parsley and salt and pepper to taste. Cook over low heat, stirring frequently, 5 minutes, or until mushrooms are tender. Add spaghetti to chicken-liver mixture and toss. Serves 4.

SPECIAL
NO-PRECOOKING
PASTA RECIPES

This chapter contains recipes in which separate cooking of pasta is not required—another form of convenience.

Most are hearty soups and chowders to serve as the main course at lunch or supper. Others are soups intended to be a grand treat as a first course of any meal.

ZUPPA PASTA FAGIOLA

4 ounces (1 cup) elbow macaroni
¾ pound dried white kidney beans
Ham shank (about 2 pounds) or ham bone
2 garlic cloves, minced
4 medium-firm tomatoes, peeled and chopped
¾ teaspoon coarsely ground black pepper
¼ teaspoon ground sage
¼ teaspoon thyme
1½ quarts water
¼ cup olive oil
1 cup dry white wine
1 teaspoon salt

116

Soak beans in water overnight; drain. Remove skin and excess fat from ham shank. In a large kettle combine beans, ham shank, garlic, 2 chopped tomatoes, ½ teaspoon pepper, the sage, thyme and water. Bring to a boil; cover and simmer gently 2 hours, or until beans are tender. Remove shank from kettle; dice meat and return to soup.

Meanwhile, in medium saucepan, combine olive oil, remaining 2 chopped tomatoes, the wine, salt and remaining ¼ teaspoon pepper. Simmer, uncovered, 20 minutes. Pour into soup. Bring to a boil; add macaroni and cook 10 minutes longer, or until macaroni is tender. Serve in large soup bowls. Serves about 8.

MACARONI GUMBO

8 ounces (2 cups) elbow macaroni	2 bay leaves
2 garlic cloves, crushed	¼ teaspoon Tabasco
1 cup chopped onions	1 10-ounce package frozen baby okra
¼ cup butter	1 pint shucked oysters, drained
1 28-ounce can tomatoes	1 pound shrimps, shelled and cleaned
1 quart water	
2 cups clam juice	
1 tablespoon salt	1 7¾-ounce can crab meat, drained and boned
1 teaspoon orégano	

In a Dutch oven or large heavy saucepan, sauté garlic and onions in butter until golden. Add tomatoes, water, clam juice, salt, orégano, bay leaves and Tabasco. Simmer, covered, 40 minutes. Bring to a boil; gradually add macaroni, then add okra. Cook, covered, 15 minutes, or until macaroni is tender, stirring occasionally. Stir in oysters, shrimps, and crab meat. Cook 5 minutes longer. Serves 8.

METRO MINESTRONE

- 4 ounces (1 cup) elbow macaroni
- ½ pound salt pork, diced
- 5 10½-ounce cans beef broth
- 1 10-ounce package frozen peas
- 1 10-ounce package frozen lima beans
- 4 cups loosely packed fresh spinach
- 2 medium carrots, diced
- 2 medium tomatoes, diced
- ½ cup minced onion
- 1 tablespoon chopped parsley

In a large kettle, render fat from salt pork and sauté pork until lightly browned; discard drippings. Add broth to pork and bring to a boil. Add remaining ingredients and simmer, covered, 30 minutes, or until macaroni and vegetables are tender. Serves about 8.

NOODLE MINESTRONE

- 4 ounces (2 cups) ripplet egg noodles
- 2 tablespoons olive oil
- 1 large onion, chopped
- 2 quarts water
- 1 veal bone
- 1 15-ounce can red kidney beans, drained and rinsed
- 1 3-ounce can chopped mushrooms, undrained
- Salt and pepper
- 1 garlic clove, crushed
- 1 bay leaf
- 1 teaspoon orégano
- 1 medium zucchini, coarsely chopped
- 2 cups chopped escarole
- 1 pound Italian sweet sausage, sliced
- Freshly grated Parmesan cheese

In a large saucepan, heat oil and sauté onion until transparent. Add water, veal bone, kidney beans, mushrooms, salt and pepper to taste, garlic, bay leaf and orégano. Bring to a boil and simmer, covered, 45 minutes. Add zucchini, escarole, sausage and ripplets. Continue cooking, uncovered, 20 minutes. Serve with grated Parmesan cheese. Serves 6.

NOODLE EGG DROP SOUP

¾ cup fine egg noodles	2 eggs, slightly beaten
2 10½-ounce cans chicken broth, undiluted	2 tablespoons chopped parsley
1½ cups water	2 tablespoons butter

Bring chicken broth and water to a boil. Gradually add noodles, stirring occasionally; cook 10 minutes. Stir in eggs; simmer 3 minutes longer. Remove from heat. Stir in parsley and butter. Serves 4.

MACARONI MUSHROOM SOUP

1 cup salad macaroni	3 cups water
1 quart chopped mushrooms (about 1 pound)	1½ teaspoons salt
	1 teaspoon monosodium glutamate
1 cup chopped carrot	¼ teaspoon pepper
½ cup chopped onion	⅛ teaspoon nutmeg
⅓ cup chopped celery	1 quart milk
¼ cup chopped parsley	1 cup light cream
½ cup butter	½ cup sherry (optional)

Sauté vegetables in butter until crisp-tender; add water and seasonings. Bring to a boil. Gradually add pasta so that water continues to boil, stirring constantly. Reduce heat; cover tightly and simmer 5 minutes, or until pasta is tender. Add milk, cream and sherry; heat to serving temperature. Serves about 8.

NOTE: If there's any left over, this soup can be frozen. Thaw slightly and reheat in double boiler.

DOWN EAST CHOWDER

4 ounces (1 cup) elbow macaroni	1 tablespoon salt Dash of pepper
¼ cup butter	1 10-ounce package frozen chopped broccoli
½ cup chopped onion	
1 pound fish fillets, thawed	1 quart milk, scalded
2 cups hot water	½ cup light cream, scalded

Melt butter in a large saucepan. Add onion and cook until lightly browned, stirring occasionally. Cut fish into bite-size pieces. Add fish, water, salt, and pepper to onion mixture. Bring to a boil, cover, reduce heat, and simmer 15 to 20 minutes. Add broccoli and macaroni and cook 10 to 15 minutes longer, until macaroni is *al dente*. Stir in heated milk and cream. Serves 6.

MEAT BALL SOUP WITH RINGS

1 cup macaroni soup rings	2 quarts water
1 cup sliced carrots	1 egg, slightly beaten
1 cup diced celery	2 tablespoons milk
½ cup sliced green onions	1 cup fresh soft bread crumbs
¼ cup chopped parsley	
3 beef bouillon cubes	¼ cup grated Parmesan cheese
3 teaspoons salt	
1 teaspoon monosodium glutamate (optional)	1 pound ground beef round
½ teaspoon pepper	1 cup chopped fresh spinach

In a Dutch oven or kettle, combine carrots, celery, onions, parsley, bouillon cubes, 2 teaspoons salt, the monosodium glutamate, ¼ teaspoon pepper and water. Bring to a boil; reduce heat to simmer. Cover tightly and simmer 20 minutes. Meanwhile, mix together egg, milk, remaining 1 teaspoon salt and ¼ teaspoon pepper and the bread crumbs; let stand a few minutes. Stir in Parmesan and beef; mix well. Shape into 1-inch balls, about 24. Add to soup and simmer, covered, 15 minutes longer. Bring to a boil and gradually add macaroni rings; simmer uncovered until tender, about 5 minutes, stirring occasionally. Remove from heat; stir in spinach and serve. Serves 8.

HEARTY VEGETABLE SOUP

2 cups ready-cut spaghetti	2 celery ribs, cut in 1-inch pieces
3 quarts water	
2½ pounds soup bone and meat	1 large carrot, cut in 1-inch pieces
1 tablespoon salt	3 cups tomato juice
¼ teaspoon pepper	1 cup diced celery
1 bay leaf	2 cups sliced carrots

Put water, soup bone and meat, salt, pepper, bay leaf, 1-inch celery pieces and 1-inch carrot pieces in kettle. Cover and bring to a boil. Reduce heat and simmer about 2 hours. Strain and save soup stock. Remove meat from bone and cut into pieces. Add cut meat to soup stock. Then add tomato juice, diced celery and sliced carrots. Simmer 15 minutes. Add spaghetti and cook until spaghetti is tender, 10 to 15 minutes. Serves 4 to 6.

FIDEO LAREDO

12 ounces twisted vermicelli	1 medium jalapeño pepper, chopped (optional)
¼ cup butter or salad oil	
¼ cup chopped onion	½ teaspoon garlic chips
3 cups beef broth	½ teaspoon salt
1 4½-ounce can taco sauce	Grated Parmesan cheese

Melt butter in skillet. Sauté vermicelli and onion, stirring until vermicelli is browned. Combine beef broth, taco sauce, jalapeño, garlic chips and salt. Stir into vermicelli, breaking the twists apart with a spoon. Simmer uncovered, stirring constantly until vermicelli is tender and sauce is thick, about 4 minutes. Serve on a hot platter and sprinkle with Parmesan cheese. Serves 4 to 6.

BROWN BUTTERED MACARONI

8 ounces (2 cups) elbow macaroni
¼ cup butter

¼ cup chopped onion
3 cups chicken broth
1 to 2 teaspoons salt

Melt butter in skillet. Sauté macaroni and onion, stirring until macaroni is browned. Add chicken broth and salt; cover and simmer until macaroni is tender and liquid absorbed, about 20 minutes. Add additional broth if necessary. Serves 4 to 6.

HAM FIESTA

8 ounces (4 cups) wide egg noodles
3⅓ cups water
1½ cups cubed cooked ham
1 2-ounce jar pimiento strips

1 teaspoon salt
1½ teaspoons dry mustard
½ teaspoon orégano
Dash of Tabasco
1 1-pound can cream-style corn

Combine water, ham, pimientos, salt, mustard, orégano and Tabasco in a large saucepan. Heat to boiling. Add noodles gradually, so that boiling never stops. Reduce heat and simmer gently 15 minutes, stirring occasionally. Add corn and mix well. Simmer 10 minutes longer. Serves 4 to 6.

SPEEDY SPANISH NOODLES

3 cups medium egg noodles
4 slices bacon, cut in small pieces
1 cup chopped onion
1 cup chopped green pepper

1 pound ground beef
2 15-ounce cans tomatoes in purée
1 15-ounce can water
2–3 teaspoons salt

½ teaspoon orégano
Few red pepper flakes

Dash black pepper
Parmesan cheese

Fry bacon pieces until crisp. Remove and set aside. Sauté onion, green pepper and ground beef in drippings. Pour off fat. Add tomatoes, water and seasonings. Cover and simmer 10 minutes. Add noodles, a few at a time, and bring mixture to a boil. Reduce heat. Cook 10 minutes, until noodles are tender, stirring occasionally. Pour into serving dish. Top with bacon pieces and Parmesan. Serves 6 to 8.

RIGATONI WITH ONION SAUCE

4 cups rigatoni
1 1½-ounce package dry
  onion soup mix
3 cups water
1½ teaspoons salt
1 pound ground beef
  chuck

Freshly ground pepper
½ cup diced green pepper
1 pimiento, chopped
¼ cup chili sauce, or
  ¼ cup grated
  Parmesan cheese

Pour rigatoni into buttered 2-quart casserole. Sprinkle soup mix over. Add water and ½ teaspoon salt. Crumble in beef and sprinkle with remaining 1 teaspoon salt, the pepper, green pepper and pimiento. Cover tightly with lid or aluminum foil. Bake in 375° oven 50 minutes. Remove cover and spread chili sauce or grated cheese over meat. Bake, uncovered, 10 minutes longer. Serves 5 or 6.

STEWED CHICKEN WITH DUMPLINGS

8 ounces dumplings
5-pound stewing chicken,
  cut into serving pieces,
  plus giblets

½ cup salad oil
1½ quarts and 3 tablespoons
  water
1 celery rib

1 medium lemon, quartered
1 tablespoon and 2
    teaspoons salt
½ teaspoon cracked
    pepper
¾ teaspoon thyme

1 bay leaf
2 medium onions, sliced
3 cups sliced carrots
1 cup sliced celery
2 tablespoons flour

In a Dutch oven, brown chicken in oil. Drain off fat.
Add 1½ quarts water, celery rib, lemon, 1 tablespoon
salt, the pepper, thyme, bay leaf and onions to chicken
and giblets. Bring to a boil; simmer covered 1 hour, or
until chicken is tender. Remove chicken; discard chicken
skin, lemon, celery rib and bay leaf. Add 2 teaspoons salt
to chicken broth and bring to a boil; gradually add
dumplings, then carrots and sliced celery. Boil, uncovered, 15 minutes, or until dumplings and vegetables are
just tender. Stir in flour blended with 3 tablespoons water.
Cook and stir 1 minute. Add chicken and heat. Serves
6 to 8.

PRIZE-WINNING RECIPES

Cook at home like a professional with the recipes in this chapter. They are the 15 selected as "best" from among hundreds submitted by chefs for the National Pasta Contest sponsored by the National Macaroni Institute, North Dakota State Wheat Commission, and the Durum Wheat Institute. All-expense-paid trips to Europe and the Caribbean, plus generous cash prizes, were awarded for these simple but imaginative recipes.

SPAGHETTI AMERICANA "2000"

12 ounces spaghetti	3 tablespoons brandy
2 tablespoons and ¼ cup butter	8 ounces plain yogurt
¼ pound mushrooms, sliced	1 teaspoon flour
¼ cup sliced green onions	½ teaspoon salt
1 pound beef tenderloin tips, cubed	½ teaspoon sugar
⅓ cup water	¼ teaspoon nutmeg
	⅛ teaspoon white pepper

Melt 2 tablespoons butter in a saucepan or small skillet. Add mushrooms and onions; cook until just tender. Melt ¼ cup butter in a large skillet. Add tenderloin cubes and cook over medium high heat until browned. Remove meat from pan. Add water and brandy to skillet; boil rapidly 3 minutes, stirring constantly to loosen crusty bits from pan. Combine yogurt, flour and seasonings. Add to skillet; cook and stir 3 minutes. Add meat and mushroom-onion mixture; bring to serving temperature. Cook spaghetti as directed on package. Serve with sauce. Serves 6.

TEENAGER'S LASAGNE

1 pound lasagne
1 pound ground beef
½ cup chopped onion
1 garlic clove, minced
1 tablespoon oil
1 8-ounce can tomato sauce
1 6-ounce can tomato paste
1 4-ounce can sliced
   mushrooms, drained
1 teaspoon salt
½ teaspoon orégano

2 eggs, beaten
1 10-ounce package frozen
   chopped spinach,
   thawed
8 ounces small-curd
   creamed cottage cheese
½ cup sliced pitted black
   olives
8 1-ounce slices American
   cheese

Cook lasagne as directed on package. Drain. Cook beef, onion and garlic in oil until meat is browned. Stir in tomato sauce, tomato paste, mushrooms, salt and orégano. Simmer 15 minutes.

Meanwhile, combine eggs, spinach and cottage cheese. Layer ingredients in a large pan (13x9x2 inches) as follows: Pour half of tomato sauce into pan. Cover with half of lasagne. Top with all of spinach-egg mixture. Cover with remaining lasagne. Top with remaining tomato sauce. Sprinkle with sliced olives. Cover with foil. Bake in 350° oven 45 minutes. Remove foil. Arrange cheese slices over casserole; bake 15 minutes longer. Serves 6 to 8.

QUICK LASAGNE

8 ounces lasagne
1 pound ground beef

2 tablespoons butter
1 8-ounce can tomato sauce

½ teaspoon salt
1 8-ounce package cream cheese, softened

8 ounces small-curd cottage cheese
½ cup sour cream

Cook lasagne as directed on package. Drain. Brown beef in butter. Add tomato sauce and salt; simmer 5 minutes. Blend together cream cheese, cottage cheese and sour cream. Place lasagne in buttered baking dish (11x7 inches). Spread cheese mixture over lasagne; cover with meat sauce. Bake in 350° oven 30 minutes. Serves 6.

SAVORY SPAGHETTI

12 ounces spaghetti
1 pound ground beef
1 10½-ounce can tomato purée
1 12-ounce bottle chili sauce
1 1-pound can tomatoes
¼ pound mushrooms, sliced
3 tablespoons chopped parsley

3 tablespoons green pepper flakes
2 tablespoons instant minced onion
1½ teaspoons Italian seasoning
¾ teaspoon chili powder
¾ teaspoon ground cumin
½ teaspoon garlic powder
½ teaspoon onion powder

Brown ground beef in a large saucepan. Add all remaining ingredients except spaghetti. Simmer slowly 3 hours, stirring occasionally. Cook spaghetti as directed on package. Drain. Serve with sauce. Serves 6.

SPAGHETTI WITH TUNA SAUCE

12 ounces spaghetti
2 garlic cloves, minced
1 tablespoon olive oil
1 28-ounce can tomatoes, drained

2 7-ounce cans tuna, drained and flaked
1 6-ounce can tomato paste
¼ cup chopped parsley
1 teaspoon salt
¾ teaspoon pepper

Cook garlic in oil 2 minutes. Add tomatoes, tuna, tomato paste, parsley, salt and pepper. Cover and simmer 1½ hours, stirring frequently. Cook spaghetti as directed on package. Drain. Serve with sauce. Serves 6.

MACARONI SUPERB A LA HOLSTEIN

4 ounces (1 cup) elbow macaroni	1 tablespoon prepared mustard
¼ cup minced onion	1 2-ounce jar pimientos, drained and chopped
¼ cup minced green pepper	½ teaspoon salt
¼ cup butter	⅛ teaspoon white pepper
¼ cup flour	6 poached eggs
2 cups milk	
1 4-ounce package dried beef, shredded	

Cook macaroni as directed on package. Drain. Meanwhile, cook onion and green pepper in butter until soft. Blend in flour. Gradually add milk. Cook, stirring constantly, until thickened. Mix in remaining ingredients except eggs. Pour into buttered 1½-quart baking dish. Bake in 350° oven 25 to 30 minutes. Top individual servings with poached eggs, if desired. Serves 6.

SPAGHETTI WITH CRAB SAUCE

12 ounces spaghetti	¼ cup chopped parsley
1 cup coarsely chopped celery	½ teaspoon salt
½ cup chopped onion	¼ teaspoon pepper
3 garlic cloves, minced	¼ teaspoon paprika
¼ cup olive oil	1 pound canned or thawed frozen crab meat, drained and flaked
2 8-ounce cans tomato sauce	Grated Parmesan cheese
1 cup drained, diced canned tomatoes	

Cook celery, onion and garlic in oil until tender. Stir in tomato sauce, tomatoes, parsley and seasonings; simmer, covered, 25 minutes. Mix in crab meat; heat through. Cook spaghetti as directed on package. Drain. Serve with sauce and sprinkle with cheese. Serves 6.

CHINESE LOBSTER MACARONI

8 ounces (2 cups) elbow macaroni
2 cups lobster chunks (two 8- or 9-ounce packages frozen lobster tails, thawed)
1 pound ground pork
¼ cup oil
1 quart chicken broth

¼ cup soy sauce
2 tablespoons sugar
2 tablespoons monosodium glutamate
1 teaspoon salt
1 large garlic clove, minced
¾ cup cold water
½ cup cornstarch
¼ cup sliced green onions

Cook lobster and pork in oil until pork is lightly browned. Stir in chicken broth; bring to a boil. Add soy sauce, sugar, monosodium glutamate, salt and garlic. Combine water and cornstarch; gradually add to meat mixture, stirring constantly. Simmer, stirring constantly, until thickened. Cook macaroni as directed on package. Drain. Serve with sauce, garnish with onions. Serves 6.

JEFFERSON HOUSE SPECKLED NOODLES

8 ounces (4 cups) medium egg noodles
¼ cup butter
2 tablespoons poppy seeds
2 tablespoons sesame seeds
1 tablespoon caraway or dill seeds

½ cup chopped stuffed green olives
½ teaspoon salt
¼ teaspoon coarse black pepper

Cook noodles as directed on package. Drain. Melt butter; add seeds and cook until sesame seeds are lightly browned. Add noodles and remaining ingredients; toss. Serves 6.

SOUR CREAM NOODLE BAKE

8 ounces (4 cups) medium
  egg noodles
1 pound ground beef
1 tablespoon butter
1 8-ounce can tomato sauce
1 teaspoon salt
¼ teaspoon garlic salt

⅛ teaspoon pepper
2 cups sour cream
1 cup thinly sliced green
  onions
1 cup shredded Cheddar
  cheese

Cook noodles as directed on package. Drain. Brown beef
in butter. Stir in tomato sauce, salt, garlic salt and pepper. Simmer, uncovered, 5 minutes. Mix together sour
cream, onions and noodles. In buttered 2-quart casserole,
alternate layers of noodle and meat mixtures, beginning
with noodles and ending with meat. Sprinkle with
cheese. Bake in 350° oven 20 to 25 minutes, or until
cheese is lightly browned. Serves 6.

NOODLE AND SQUASH CASSEROLE

8 ounces (4 cups) wide
  egg noodles
3 tablespoons melted
  butter
2 tablespoons flour
1 teaspoon salt
⅛ teaspoon white pepper

2 cups milk
1 cup cubed Cheddar
  cheese
1 cup cubed Swiss cheese
1½ pounds zucchini, sliced
½ cup fine dry bread
  crumbs

Heat 2 tablespoons butter in a saucepan. Blend in flour,
salt and pepper. Gradually add milk, stirring constantly.
Cook over medium heat, stirring constantly, until thickened. Add cheeses; stir until melted. Cook noodles as
directed on package. Drain. Spread half of noodles over
bottom of buttered 9-inch-square pan. Arrange half of
zucchini slices over noodles and pour half of cheese
sauce on top. Repeat layers. Mix together bread crumbs
and remaining butter; sprinkle over noodle mixture. Bake

in 350° oven 30 minutes, or until golden brown. Serves 6 to 8.

SEACOAST SALAD

8 ounces shell macaroni
2 grapefruit
2 tablespoons salad oil
½ teaspoon salt
¼ teaspoon dry mustard
⅛ teaspoon white pepper
⅔ cup cooked shrimp pieces
⅓ cup flaked cooked crab meat
¼ cup cubed cooked lobster
½ cup cooked cut green beans
2 tablespoons chopped green pepper
2 tablespoons sliced celery
1 medium head lettuce
French or Italian dressing

Peel grapefruit and section, reserving sections and juice. Squeeze juice from membranes and reserve also. Prepare marinade by combining ½ cup grapefruit juice, the salad oil, salt, mustard and white pepper. Add seafood and mix. Cover and refrigerate several hours or overnight, stirring once or twice.

Cook macaroni as directed on the package. Drain. Cool. Combine macaroni, green beans, green pepper, celery and reserved grapefruit sections. Drain seafood; discard marinade. Toss seafood with macaroni mixture; chill. Remove outer leaves of lettuce to make 6 lettuce cups; place in large individual salad bowls. Shred remaining lettuce and divide among bowls. Fill bowls with macaroni mixture and top with dressing. Serves 6.

GODDESS CHICKEN SALAD

8 ounces shell macaroni
2 cups cubed cooked chicken
¾ cup thinly sliced celery
½ cup Green Goddess dressing
⅓ cup thinly sliced radishes
¼ cup sour cream
1 small red onion, sliced and separated into rings

1 2-ounce jar pimientos,
    drained and chopped
½ teaspoon salt

½ teaspoon pepper
6 slices bacon
6 tomatoes

Cook macaroni as directed on package. Drain. Cool. Combine macaroni with remaining ingredients except bacon and tomatoes. Chill thoroughly. Cook bacon until done but not crisp. Roll up each slice with a fork to form a curl. Cut stem end out of tomatoes. Cut tomatoes into eighths, cutting almost to, but not through, bottom. Gently open tomato "flowers"; fill with chilled macaroni mixture; garnish with bacon curls. Serves 6.

LASAGNE CAESAR SALAD

8 ounces lasagne
1 garlic clove
1 egg yolk
    Salad Dressing (below)
2 quarts torn or cut
    Romaine lettuce

2 cups garlic flavored
    croutons
¼ cup grated Parmesan
    cheese

Rub a large bowl with cut clove of garlic. Cook lasagne as directed on package. Drain. Cool. Cut lasagne into strips (¼x2 inches); put in a bowl. Add egg yolk to lasagne strips and toss. Pour on salad dressing and mix thoroughly. Add lettuce, 1 cup croutons and 2 table-spoons cheese; toss. Sprinkle with remaining croutons and cheese. Serves 6.

Salad Dressing:

½ cup oil
2½ tablespoons white
    vinegar
1 garlic clove, minced
1 teaspoon salt

½ teaspoon anchovy paste
½ teaspoon sugar
¼ teaspoon black pepper
⅛ teaspoon dry mustard

Combine ingredients in a small bowl and blend thoroughly.

GARDEN FRESH SALAD

12 ounces macaroni rings	1½ cups mayonnaise
1 10-ounce package frozen mixed vegetables	1 teaspoon salt
	1 teaspoon onion salt
1½ cups diced Cheddar cheese	½ teaspoon pepper
	Lettuce leaves

Cook macaroni as directed on package. Drain. Cool. Cook vegetables as directed on package. Drain. Cool. Combine macaroni, vegetables, cheese, mayonnaise and seasonings. Chill. Serve on lettuce leaves. Serves 10 to 12.

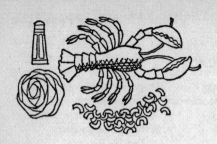

FROZEN PASTA

Frozen egg noodles: a newcomer to look for in your grocer's freezer. This pasta product, with a homemade flavor and texture, saves hours of preparation. Ask anyone who has ever made homemade noodles!

The recipes in this chapter are especially suited to frozen noodles, but you may substitute regular noodles. Likewise, frozen egg noodles can be used in the other recipes in this book. Be sure to try these new taste delights.

QUICK MEAT BALL STROGANOFF

16 ounces frozen egg noodles	1 tablespoon parsley flakes
1½ pounds ground beef chuck	2 tablespoons salad oil
¾ cup fine bread crumbs	1 ½-ounce envelope beef stroganoff sauce mix
1½ teaspoons salt	½ cup water
¼ teaspoon pepper	¼ cup sherry (optional)
	1 cup sour cream

Cook noodles (do not thaw first) as directed on package. Drain. Meanwhile, combine beef, bread crumbs, salt, pepper and parsley. Shape into 1¼-inch balls. In a large skillet, heat oil and sauté meat balls until browned. Push to sides of skillet. Blend sauce mix, water and sherry; stir into skillet. Cover and simmer 10 minutes. Stir in sour cream; heat, but *do not boil.* Serve over noodles. Serves 6 to 8.

BEEF STROGANOFF DELIGHT

- 8 ounces frozen egg noodles
- 1½ pounds round steak, cut in strips about ¼x½x2 inches
- 1 medium onion, chopped
- 3 tablespoons butter
- 1 10½-ounce can condensed cream of celery (or mushroom) soup
- 1 10½-ounce can condensed beef bouillon
- ¼ cup flour blended in 2 tablespoons water
- 1 2-ounce can mushroom pieces
- 1 cup sour cream

Sauté meat and onion in butter until meat is browned. Combine soup with beef bouillon and add to meat; cover, and simmer until meat is tender, about 45 minutes. Stir occasionally. About 30 minutes before serving, cook noodles (do not thaw first) as directed on package. Drain. Blend flour with water and stir into meat mixture to thicken gravy. Add mushrooms, including juice, and stir in sour cream. Heat to serving temperature; do not boil. Serve meat and gravy over hot noodles. Serves 6.

ITALIAN-STYLE SHORT RIBS

- 8 ounces frozen egg noodles
- 3 pounds short ribs, cut into 2-inch pieces
- Seasoned flour
- 2 tablespoons salad oil
- 1 medium onion, chopped
- 1 cup chopped celery
- 1 garlic clove, minced
- 1 cup beer or water

1 8-ounce can plum
tomatoes
1½ teaspoons salt
1 teaspoon Italian
seasoning
¼ teaspoon lemon and
pepper seasoning

¼ teaspoon basil
1 tablespoon butter
1 tablespoon chopped
parsley

Dredge short ribs with seasoned flour. In a Dutch oven, brown ribs well in hot oil. Remove ribs and discard excess fat. Add onion, celery and garlic to remaining fat and sauté 2 minutes. Add beer and stir to scrape brown particles loose. Add tomatoes, salt and seasonings. Return ribs. Cover and simmer 1½ hours, or until tender.

About 30 minutes before serving, cook noodles (do not thaw first) as directed on package. Drain. Toss with butter and parsley. Serve with short ribs and gravy. Thicken gravy with a little flour if desired. Serves 4.

LASAGNE-STYLE NOODLE CASSEROLE

16 ounces frozen egg
noodles
2 tablespoons salad or olive
oil
1 pound ground beef
½ cup chopped onion
¾ teaspoon garlic salt
½ teaspoon orégano

2 15-ounce cans tomato
sauce
3 cups drained cottage or
ricotta cheese
8 ounces sliced mozzarella
or brick cheese
½ cup grated Parmesan
cheese

Cook noodles (do not thaw first) according to package directions. Drain. Sauté and stir ground beef and onion in hot oil until meat loses pink color. Blend in garlic salt, orégano and tomato sauce. Remove from heat. Place half of noodles in buttered baking dish (13x9x2 inches). Add half of meat sauce, cottage cheese and mozzarella. Repeat layers and top with Parmesan. Bake uncovered in 350° oven until piping hot, about 35 minutes. Serves 8 to 12.

PORK TENDERLOIN WITH NOODLES

8 ounces frozen egg
   noodles

1½ pounds pork tenderloin,
   cut in 1-inch slices and
   flattened

Salt and pepper

Flour

3 tablespoons salad oil

2 tablespoons chopped
   onion

2 tablespoons chopped
   celery

1 4-ounce can mushrooms

1¼ cups chicken broth

1 tablespoon
   Worcestershire

Sprinkle pork tenderloin lightly with salt and pepper, then turn in flour. Pan fry slowly in oil until meat is browned; remove meat from pan and sauté onion and celery. Add mushrooms with liquid and chicken broth. Stir, add browned pork, cover, and simmer over low heat until meat is tender, about 1 hour. Stir in Worcestershire and let simmer, uncovered, for about 10 minutes. About 30 minutes before serving, cook egg noodles (do not thaw first) as directed on package. Drain. Place pork tenderloin on platter and ring with noodles. Pour gravy over all. Serves 6.

CHICKEN VEGETABLE CASSEROLE

8 ounces frozen egg
   noodles

3 cups diced cooked chicken
   or 3 5-ounce cans
   chicken

1 10½-ounce can condensed
   cream of chicken soup

1 10-ounce package frozen
   peas and carrots

½ cup diced celery

1 tablespoon green pepper
   flakes

¼ cup chopped pimientos

1 tablespoon instant
   minced onion

1 4-ounce can mushrooms,
   drained

2 hard-cooked eggs, sliced

Combine all ingredients except noodles and egg slices in 2-quart casserole. Cover and bake in 350° oven 30 to 45 minutes, until piping hot. Meanwhile, cook noodles (do

not thaw first) as directed on package. Drain. Serve with
chicken mixture and garnish with egg slices. Serves 6.

GRANDMA'S CHICKEN FRICASSEE WITH NOODLES

16 ounces frozen egg noodles	1½ teaspoons salt
1 4- to 4½-pound stewing chicken	⅛ teaspoon pepper
	2 teaspoons bouquet garni
5 cups water (or enough to barely cover chicken)	Paprika

Cut chicken into serving pieces. Place in Dutch oven or
heavy saucepan; add water and seasonings, cover, and
simmer until fork-tender; allow 2 to 3 hours; time will
vary with the bird. Add small quantity of hot water
when necessary. When chicken is tender, remove pieces
from broth. Measure 5 cups of broth; add water if necessary to make the 5 cups. Bring to a boil and add egg
noodles; cook (do not thaw first) as directed on package.
Return chicken pieces to noodle mixture and cook over
low heat about 15 minutes. Serve in a large bowl. Sprinkle
with paprika. Serves 8.

OLD-FASHIONED CHICKEN 'N' NOODLES

16 ounces frozen egg noodles	3 carrots, sliced
5 cups water	1 small onion, sliced
1 3-pound broiler-fryer chicken, cut in serving pieces	3 celery ribs, sliced
	2 tablespoons chopped parsley
1 tablespoon salt	1 4-ounce can mushroom stems and pieces, undrained
⅛ teaspoon pepper	

Add chicken, salt and pepper to water in tightly covered
pan. Bring to a boil, then simmer 1 hour, or until chicken
is tender. Remove chicken from broth and keep warm.

Measure broth, adding enough hot water to make 6 cups of liquid. Return broth to pan; add noodles (do not thaw first) and remaining ingredients. Stir until noodles are defrosted and thoroughly separated. After liquid returns to a boil, simmer, stirring occasionally, an additional 25 minutes, or until noodles and vegetables are almost tender. Add chicken and heat 10 minutes more. Serves 6 to 8.

SKILLET TUNA SUPREME

8 ounces frozen egg noodles
1 cup diagonally sliced celery
¼ cup finely sliced green onions
1 small green pepper, diced
2 tablespoons butter
1 3-ounce can mushrooms
3 tablespoons cooking sherry

1 6½- or 7-ounce can tuna, drained and flaked
½ teaspoon salt
⅛ teaspoon cracked black pepper
¼ teaspoon marjoram
¼ cup heavy cream
1 pimiento, diced
½ cup slivered almonds

Cook noodles (do not thaw first) as directed on package. Drain. Meanwhile, sauté celery, onions and green pepper in butter until crisp-tender. Add mushrooms with liquid, sherry, tuna, salt, pepper and marjoram. Reduce heat, cover and cook 5 minutes. Stir in cream. Remove from heat and spoon over noodles. Garnish with pimiento and almonds. Serves 4.

CHINESE-STYLE CHICKEN AND NOODLES

8 ounces frozen egg noodles
2 cups diced cooked chicken
½ pound fresh mushrooms, sliced

3 tablespoons butter
2 teaspoons arrowroot or cornstarch
2 tablespoons green pepper flakes

2 tablespoons chicken-
  seasoned stock base
3 cups hot water
2 tablespoons soy sauce
1 5-ounce can water
  chestnuts, drained and
  sliced

2 tablespoons instant
  toasted onions
¼ cup slivered toasted
  almonds

Cook noodles (do not thaw first) as directed on package. Drain. Combine with chicken in 2-quart casserole. Cook mushrooms in butter until tender. Stir in arrowroot, green pepper flakes, chicken stock base and water; cook until sauce begins to boil. Stir in soy sauce, water chestnuts and onions. Pour over noodles and chicken and mix well. Sprinkle with almonds. Bake in 350° oven 20 to 30 minutes, or until piping hot. Serves 6. (*This recipe courtesy of Spice Islands, Inc.*)

BAVARIAN CREAMED EGG NOODLES

16 ounces frozen egg
  noodles
1 10½-ounce can condensed
  cream of mushroom
  soup

½ cup milk
½ teaspoon parsley flakes
¼ teaspoon salt
6 hard-cooked eggs, diced

Cook noodles (do not thaw first) as directed on package. Drain. Blend soup and milk. Stir in noodles with seasonings. Gently mix in diced eggs. Stir and warm over very low heat about 5 minutes. Serves 6 to 8.

GOLDEN GATE SHRIMP BAKE

8 ounces frozen egg
  noodles
½ pound mushrooms, sliced
6 tablespoons butter
1 teaspoon curry powder

2 to 3 tablespoons chicken-
  seasoned stock base
2 tablespoons dry white
  wine
2 cups sour cream

1½ cups shredded sharp
  Cheddar cheese
2 4-ounce cans shrimps,
  drained and rinsed

½ cup chopped green
  onions
1 avocado, peeled and
  diced

Cook noodles (do not thaw first) as directed on package. Drain. Meanwhile, sauté mushrooms in butter. Stir in curry powder and chicken stock base. Remove from heat. Add wine; blend in sour cream and 1 cup shredded cheese. Stir shrimps, onions and avocado into sour-cream mixture. Toss lightly with noodles and turn into 1½-quart casserole. Sprinkle with remaining ½ cup shredded cheese. Bake in 375° oven 25 to 30 minutes, until cheese is melted and casserole bubbly. Serves 4. (*This recipe courtesy of Spice Islands, Inc.*)

CALORIE-CUTTING PASTA DISHES AND WEIGHT-CONTROL MENUS

A good reducing diet meets nutritional needs. Since it is the total number of calories consumed that determines whether you will gain or lose, by careful planning you can include pasta in any weight-control diet. Doing so will give you plenty of stamina to get through the day.

For example, 2 ounces of uncooked macaroni represents one adult weight-control serving (about 200 calories) which, when cooked, yields about 1 cup. This is modest enough considering the other valuable nutrients that pasta furnishes *(see Appendix)*. When combined with vegetables and nominal amounts of other protein-rich foods like lean meat, cheese, milk or eggs, pasta provides a nutritious, filling main dish.

By utilizing various combinations of spices and herbs, by carefully balancing the other foods, and by changing the size and shape of the pasta product, you can put together a balanced regimen of low-calorie meals that you will enjoy eating all the more because they will help you lose weight without any risk to your health.

The menus that follow, each with a main-dish pasta recipe, have been developed to demonstrate how easily you can put together such meals. Most pasta products are enriched; they supply essential vitamins and iron, as well as valuable protein and carbohydrates (*see appendix*).

Enjoy good eating and good health while you strive for a new, slimmer you!

SUMMER SALAD SPECIAL MENU

	Calories
Shrimp Cocktail (6 medium canned)	35
Chili Sauce (1 tablespoon)	20
MACARONI GARDEN SALAD (1 serving)	229
Angel Cake (1-inch section of 8-inch cake)	55
Fresh Strawberries (½ cup)	30
Skim Milk (1 cup)	90
Total calories approximately:	459

MACARONI GARDEN SALAD

8 ounces (2 cups) elbow macaroni
1 cup creamed cottage cheese
1 cucumber, thinly sliced
12 radishes, thinly sliced
½ cup diced celery
1 tablespoon chopped onion
1 teaspoon salt
½ teaspoon dry mustard
3 tablespoons French dressing
1 medium head Boston lettuce

Cook macaroni as directed on package. Drain. Cool. Combine remaining ingredients except lettuce; toss with macaroni. Chill. Serve salad in lettuce-lined bowl. Serves 6.

HURRY CURRY MENU

	Calories
CURRIED TURKEY WITH NOODLES (1 serving)	290
Asparagus (6 medium spears, cooked)	20
Coleslaw (½ cup)	60
Apple (1 medium, raw)	70
Skim Milk	90
Total calories approximately:	530

CURRIED TURKEY WITH NOODLES

8 ounces (4 cups) medium egg noodles
1 medium onion, chopped
1 cup sliced celery
1 tablespoon curry powder
2 tablespoons butter
2 tablespoons flour

3 chicken bouillon cubes
2 cups water
½ teaspoon garlic salt
1 tablespoon lemon juice
2 cups diced cooked turkey (light meat)
1 cup grated carrots

Cook noodles as directed on package. Drain. Meanwhile, sauté onion and celery with curry powder in butter over low heat until vegetables are crisp-tender. Mix in flour and bouillon cubes. Gradually add water; cook, stirring constantly, until sauce boils 1 minute. Stir in garlic salt, lemon juice, turkey and carrots. Serve over noodles. Garnish with chopped parsley, if desired. Serves 6.

MACARONI CHEESE SUPPER MENU

	Calories
Chicken Bouillon (1 cup)	30
MACARONI AND CHEESE (1 serving)	356
Asparagus (6 medium spears, cooked)	20
Sliced Tomatoes (½ medium)	18
Fresh Strawberries (½ cup)	30
Skim Milk (1 cup)	90
Total calories approximately:	544

MACARONI AND CHEESE

8 ounces (2 cups) elbow
macaroni
3 tablespoons butter
3 tablespoons flour
1 teaspoon salt

1½ cups milk
1½ cups grated process
Cheddar cheese
(6 ounces)

Cook macaroni as directed on package. Drain. Meanwhile, melt butter over low heat. Blend in flour and salt. Gradually add milk and 1 cup of the cheese. Cook over low heat, stirring constantly, until sauce is thickened and cheese melted. Add cooked macaroni; mix well. Turn into buttered 2-quart casserole. Sprinkle remaining cheese over top. Bake in 375° oven about 20 minutes. Serves 6.

WAIST WATCHERS' SPAGHETTI SUPPER MENU

	Calories
SPAGHETTI WITH TUNA SAUCE	330
Green Beans (½ cup, cooked)	15
Mushrooms (¼ cup, canned solids and liquid)	10
Sliced Tomatoes with Orégano (½ medium)	18
Banana with Cinnamon (1 medium, sliced)	85
Skim Milk (1 cup)	90
Total calories approximately:	548

SPAGHETTI WITH TUNA SAUCE

8 ounces thin spaghetti
1 teaspoon salad oil
½ cup chopped celery
leaves
1 4-ounce can mushroom
slices, drained
1 medium onion, chopped

1 teaspoon orégano
¼ teaspoon garlic salt
1 tablespoon flour
1½ cups clam-tomato juice
1 6½- or 7-ounce can water-
packed tuna, drained
and flaked

Cook spaghetti as directed on package. Drain. Meanwhile, in oil in large skillet over medium heat, sauté celery leaves, mushrooms, onion, orégano and garlic salt until onion is tender. Stir in flour until blended; stir in clam-tomato juice. Reduce heat and simmer 10 minutes. Add tuna; simmer 5 minutes more. Toss tuna sauce with spaghetti. Serves 4.

VEAL CUTLET DINNER MENU

	Calories
VEAL CUTLET-MACARONI DINNER	
(1 serving)	327
Tossed Salad (4 large lettuce leaves, shredded)	20
¼ green pepper and 2 radishes, sliced	4
1 tablespoon blue cheese dressing	80
Unsweetened Applesauce (½ cup)	50
Skim Milk (1 cup)	90
Total calories approximately:	571

VEAL CUTLET-MACARONI DINNER

1 cup elbow macaroni	1 cup tomato purée
1 garlic clove, chopped	1 1-pound can tomatoes
1 medium onion, chopped	1 teaspoon salt
1½ teaspoons butter	1 teaspoon orégano
4 3-ounce boned veal	Dash of pepper
cutlets	Parsley

Sauté garlic and onion in butter. Add veal cutlets and brown on both sides. Stir in tomato purée, tomatoes, salt, orégano and pepper. Cook over low heat, stirring occasionally, until veal is tender, about 30 minutes. Meanwhile, cook macaroni as directed on package. Drain. Arrange on hot serving platter. Top with veal cutlets, sauce and parsley. Serves 4.

MILANESE SPAGHETTI DINNER MENU

	Calories
Antipasto:	
Radishes (2 small)	3
Celery (2 ribs, 5-inch length)	7
Carrot Sticks (¼ medium)	5
Green Pepper Rings (¼ medium)	3
SPAGHETTI MILANESE	412
Grapefruit (½ medium)	55
Skim milk (1 cup)	90
Total calories approximately:	575

SPAGHETTI MILANESE

8 ounces spaghetti
¾ pound ground lean beef
2 garlic cloves, finely chopped
1 small onion, chopped
1 19-ounce can tomatoes
1 6-ounce can tomato paste
½ cup canned sliced mushrooms
1½ teaspoons orégano
¼ teaspoon pepper
½ teaspoon salt

In a skillet, slowly brown beef, stirring frequently. Add garlic and onion and cook until tender. Add tomatoes, tomato paste, mushrooms, orégano, pepper and salt; simmer covered 1 hour. Cook spaghetti as directed on package. Drain. Pour sauce over spaghetti. Serves 4.

MACARONI PATIO SPECIAL MENU

	Calories
Tomato Soup (1 cup)	90
MACARONI SALMON SALAD (1 serving)	336
Cantaloupe (½, 5-inch diameter)	60
Skim Milk (1 cup)	90
Total calories approximately:	576

MACARONI SALMON SALAD

8 ounces (2 cups) elbow
   macaroni
1 1-pound can salmon
1 cup seeded and diced
   cucumber
½ cup chopped green
   pepper
½ cup chopped onion
1 cup chopped celery

1 cup low-calorie
   mayonnaise
1 teaspoon salt
½ teaspoon coarsely
   ground pepper
1½ teaspoons dillweed
Chilled lettuce
2 hard-cooked eggs,
   quartered

Cook macaroni as directed on package. Drain. Cool. Drain salmon; remove skin and center bone; flake slightly. Toss with macaroni, vegetables, mayonnaise and seasonings in large bowl; cover and chill thoroughly. Spoon salad into lettuce-lined bowl. Garnish with egg quarters. Serves 6.

GOURMET MEAT BALL DINNER MENU

	Calories
HUNGARIAN MEAT BALLS WITH NOODLES (1 serving)	422
Peas (½ cup, cooked)	60
Tomato Salad (1 medium tomato, sliced, 5 cucumber slices, low-calorie dressing)	40
Grapefruit (½ medium, broiled)	55
Black Coffee or Tea	—
Total calories approximately:	577

HUNGARIAN MEAT BALLS WITH NOODLES

8 ounces (4 cups) egg
   noodles
¾ pound ground lean beef
¼ cup chopped parsley
2 tablespoons chopped
   onion

1 teaspoon salt
½ teaspoon paprika
2 tablespoons olive oil
2 cups water
1 chicken bouillon cube
Salt and pepper

Combine ground beef, parsley, onion, salt and paprika. Mix well. Shape into 1-inch balls. Heat olive oil in skillet. Add meat balls and cook until browned on all sides. Stir in water and bouillon cube and bring to a boil. Cover and simmer 20 minutes. Cook noodles as directed on package. Drain. Arrange in serving dish. Lift meat balls from liquid and place on top of noodles. Season liquid with salt and pepper to taste. Pour over noodles. Serves 4.

MANDARIN MINI-DINNER MENU

	Calories
MACARONI ORIENTAL (1 serving)	345
Fruit Salad (1 small slice canned pineapple)	45
1 fresh tangerine, medium size	40
½ cup fresh grapes	50
lettuce cup	5
2 teaspoons French dressing	40
Fig Bar (1 small)	55
Black Coffee or Tea	—
Total calories approximately:	580

MACARONI ORIENTAL (low calorie)

8 ounces (2 cups) elbow macaroni

1 10-ounce package fresh or frozen leaf spinach

1 4-ounce can whole mushrooms

2 beef bouillon cubes

1 pound thinly sliced beef sirloin, cut in strips

2 tablespoons butter

1 small Bermuda onion, sliced

6 green onions, cut in 1-inch pieces

2 cups diagonally sliced celery

1 5-ounce can water chestnuts, drained and sliced

1 tablespoon cornstarch

¼ cup soy sauce

Prepare fresh spinach for cooking, or defrost frozen spinach in hot water. Measure liquid from mushrooms.

Add enough water to make 1 cup. Heat to boiling and stir in bouillon cubes. Start cooking macaroni as directed on package. Drain. Meanwhile, in a large skillet, sauté beef in butter until lightly browned. Add drained spinach, mushrooms, onions, celery, water chestnuts and bouillon. Cook covered 3 minutes. Blend cornstarch with soy sauce. Stir into skillet and boil 1 minute. Serve over hot macaroni with additional soy sauce, if desired. Serves 6.

CHICKEN DINNER MENU

	Calories
CHICKEN AND NOODLES EN BIANCO (1 serving)	408
Salad:	
Lettuce Wedge (⅙ medium head)	12
Low-Calorie Salad Dressing (3 tablespoons)	45
Blueberries (½ cup raw)	40
Skim Milk (1 cup)	90
Total calories approximately:	595

CHICKEN AND NOODLES EN BIANCO

8 ounces (4 cups) medium egg noodles
2 cups chicken broth or bouillon
¼ cup cold water
3 tablespoons flour
¼ to ½ teaspoon salt
¼ teaspoon pepper
¼ teaspoon tarragon
1 10-ounce package frozen peas and carrots, cooked and drained
2 cups diced, cooked chicken
1 tablespoon chopped parsley

Cook noodles as directed on package. Drain. Bring broth to a boil. Gradually blend water into flour to form a smooth paste. Gradually stir into boiling broth, stirring constantly until mixture boils 1 minute. Add seasonings; stir in vegetables and chicken. Heat to serving temperature; toss with noodles. Garnish with parsley. Serves 4.

SLIM-DOWN NOODLE DINNER MENU

	Calories
NOODLE AND HAM CASSEROLE	419
Broccoli (½ cup, chopped)	20
Lemon wedge (⅙ medium)	3
Carrot Salad (½ cup grated)	23
Lettuce (1 large leaf)	5
Grapefruit (½ cup sections)	38
Skim Milk (1 cup)	90
Total calories approximately:	598

NOODLE AND HAM CASSEROLE

8 ounces (4 cups) wide egg noodles

1 cup chicken bouillon or stock

2 cups diced cooked ham

1 3-ounce can sliced mushrooms

¼ cup non-fat dry milk crystals

1 teaspoon dry mustard

1 teaspoon onion salt

1 teaspoon butter

Cook noodles as directed on package. Drain. Meanwhile, mix together bouillon, ham, undrained mushrooms, dry-milk crystals, mustard and onion salt. Add noodles; mix well. Turn noodle mixture into buttered 2-quart casserole and bake in 350° oven 1 hour. Serves 4.

BURGER BASH MENU

	Calories
Jellied Consommé (½ cup)	15
FESTIVE EGG NOODLES AND BURGERS (1 serving)	466
Fresh Pineapple (⅓ cup, diced, raw)	27
Skim Milk (1 cup)	90
Total calories approximately:	598

FESTIVE EGG NOODLES AND BURGERS

8 ounces (4 cups) wide egg
    noodles
Burgers
2 tablespoons butter
2 cups diced green peppers

½ cup thinly sliced green
    onions
¼ cup diced pimientos
2 tablespoons low-calorie
    Italian dressing
Salt and pepper

Prepare burgers: Combine 1 pound ground lean beef, 1 teaspoon salt, 2 teaspoons prepared mustard, ⅛ teaspoon pepper and ¼ cup chopped parsley in bowl; mix lightly and shape into 4 patties. Broil 3 inches from source of heat 5 minutes on each side, or to desired doneness.

Cook noodles as directed on package. Drain. Meanwhile, melt butter in saucepan over medium heat. Add green peppers and green onions and sauté until tender. Stir in pimientos and dressing. Toss with noodles; add salt and pepper to taste. Serve with burgers. Serves 4.

TRIM LINE MACARONI MEAL MENU

	Calories
MACARONI CHICKEN SALAD (1 serving)	477
Fresh Strawberries (⅔ cup)	33
Skim Milk (1 cup)	90
Total calories approximately:	600

MACARONI CHICKEN SALAD

8 ounces (2 cups) elbow
    macaroni
2 cups diced cooked chicken
1 cup diced celery
2 sweet gherkins, chopped
2 tablespoons chopped
    onion

1 canned pimiento, chopped
⅓ cup mayonnaise
Juice of 1 medium lemon
⅛ teaspoon dry mustard
Dash of Tabasco
1 medium tomato, cut in 8
    wedges

Cook macaroni as directed on package. Drain. Cool. Combine and toss macaroni, chicken, celery, gherkins, onion, pimiento, mayonnaise, lemon juice and seasonings. Chill. Garnish with tomato wedges. Serves 4.

SAVORY STEAK DINNER MENU

	Calories
HERB SPAGHETTI WITH MINUTE STEAK (1 serving)	490
Celery (2 small ribs, 5-inch length)	10
Peaches (½ cup slices, canned)	100
Black Coffee or Tea	—
Total calories approximately:	600

HERB SPAGHETTI WITH MINUTE STEAK

8 ounces spaghetti
⅓ cup chopped green pepper
¼ cup slivered ripe olives
2 tablespoons chopped onion
2 tablespoons butter
1 1-pound can tomatoes

1 teaspoon brown sugar
½ teaspoon celery salt
¼ teaspoon crushed orégano
¼ teaspoon crushed basil
4 4-ounce minute steaks
Salt and pepper
3 tablespoons grated Parmesan cheese

Cook pepper, olives and onion in 1 tablespoon butter for 3 minutes. Add tomatoes, sugar and seasonings. Cover and simmer 20 minutes. Meanwhile, cook spaghetti as directed on package. Drain. Circle hot serving platter with spaghetti. Spoon most of the herb sauce over spaghetti, leaving small amount in pan. Keep platter hot in low-temperature oven. Season steaks with salt and pepper. Stir remaining butter into pan and quickly cook steaks, browning on both sides. Arrange steaks in center

of platter. Sprinkle cheese over herb-sauced spaghetti.
Serves 4.

BEEF-NOODLE CURRY
(About 290 calories per serving)

2 ounces (1 cup) wide egg noodles	1 medium onion, chopped
	1 garlic clove, crushed
¾ pound beef round, cut in 1-inch cubes	1 tablespoon curry powder
	1 teaspoon salt
1½ teaspoons butter	Dash of pepper

Brown beef on all sides in butter. Add onion and sauté
until onion is lightly browned. Add water to cover and
heat to boiling. Cover, and simmer 1½ hours, or until
meat is tender. Add garlic, curry powder, salt and pepper.
Cook 15 minutes, stirring occasionally. Cook noodles as
directed on package. Drain. Serve curry over noodles.
Serves 4.

NOODLES AND CHICKEN LIVERS
(About 302 calories per serving)

2 ounces (1 cup) medium egg noodles	2 chicken bouillon cubes
	1 cup water
1½ teaspoons butter	½ teaspoon Worcestershire
1 pound chicken livers	Salt and pepper
1½ teaspoons flour	

Cook noodles as directed on package. Drain. Meanwhile,
melt butter. Add livers and cook until browned on all
sides. Add flour and blend. Add bouillon cubes. Gradually
add water and cook over low heat, stirring constantly,
until slightly thickened. Add Worcestershire and salt and
pepper to taste. Serve mixture over noodles. Serves 4.

MACARONI SPRING SALAD
(About 325 calories per serving)

8 ounces (2 cups) elbow
    macaroni
2 6½-ounce cans crab meat,
    boned
1 medium onion, chopped
1 medium cucumber, sliced
½ cup sliced celery
⅓ cup chopped radishes
1 large carrot, grated
½ cup low-calorie Italian
    salad dressing
⅓ cup chili sauce
¼ cup lemon juice
1 tablespoon Worcestershire
Salt and pepper
6 hard-cooked eggs, halved

Cook macaroni as directed on package. Drain. Cool. In a large bowl combine macaroni, crab meat, vegetables, salad dressing, chili sauce, lemon juice, Worcestershire and salt and pepper to taste; toss lightly. Chill; garnish with egg halves before serving. Surround with salad greens, if desired. Serves 6.

PIQUANT MACARONI SALAD
(About 330 calories per serving)

8 ounces (2 cups) elbow
    macaroni
2 cups boiling water
½ cup wine vinegar
1 medium onion, sliced
3½ teaspoons salt
1 teaspoon pickling spices
3 peppercorns
2 pounds sole fillets
1 cucumber, finely diced
1 cup grated carrot
¼ teaspoon pepper
1½ cups plain yogurt
¾ cup low-calorie Italian
    dressing
Lettuce
1 medium tomato, cut in 6
    wedges

Mix boiling water, ¼ cup vinegar, onion, 2 teaspoons salt, pickling spices and peppercorns in saucepan. Add sole and cook 20 minutes, or until fish flakes easily with fork. Chill; flake.

Meanwhile, cook macaroni as directed on package. Drain. Cool. Mix together cucumber, carrot, 1½ teaspoons salt, pepper and remaining vinegar. Mix in yogurt, Italian dressing, cooked macaroni and sole. Chill thoroughly. Serve on lettuce-lined platter; garnish with tomato wedges. Serves 6.

SEASHORE SLIMMER
(About 334 calories per serving)

8 ounces vermicelli	⅛ teaspoon garlic powder
1 10-ounce can frozen condensed cream of shrimp soup	⅛ teaspoon pepper Dash of Tabasco
1 8-ounce can minced clams	¼ cup chopped parsley
⅓ cup water	2 teaspoons chopped pimientos
1 teaspoon lemon juice	

Defrost shrimp soup as directed on label. In a saucepan, blend soup, minced clams with liquid, water, lemon juice, garlic powder, pepper and Tabasco. Place over low heat until hot, about 15 minutes. Meanwhile, cook vermicelli as directed on package. Drain. Stir parsley and pimiento into sauce just before serving. Arrange vermicelli on hot platter. Spoon sauce on top. Serves 4.

SPAGHETTI WITH CHILI-FRANKFURTER SAUCE
(About 338 calories per serving)

10 ounces spaghetti	1 cup tomato purée
1 medium onion, coarsely chopped	1 1-pound can tomatoes
1 garlic clove, minced	½ teaspoon salt
1½ teaspoons butter	½ teaspoon chili powder
½ pound frankfurters, cut in quarters lengthwise	

Sauté onion and garlic in butter until lightly browned. Add frankfurters and cook until browned. Add tomato purée, tomatoes, salt and chili powder and mix well. Heat to boiling and simmer 20 minutes. Meanwhile, cook spaghetti as directed on package. Drain. Arrange on hot serving platter and pour frankfurter sauce over. Serves 6.

DIETERS' MACARONI BEEF SALAD
(About 348 calories per serving)

8 ounces (2 cups) elbow macaroni	¼ cup drained sweet pickle relish
3 cups diced cooked lean beef (about 1 pound)	2 tablespoons chopped onion
1 cup diced celery	1 teaspoon salt
1 cup low-calorie mayonnaise	⅛ teaspoon pepper
	12 small lettuce leaves

Cook macaroni as directed on package. Drain. Cool. Combine remaining ingredients except lettuce leaves; toss with macaroni. Chill. Serve each portion on 2 lettuce leaves. Serves 6.

MACARONI SALAD DELIGHT
(About 385 calories per serving)

8 ounces (2 cups) elbow macaroni	½ cup chopped celery
2 4-ounce cans Vienna sausage, drained and sliced	1 tablespoon prepared mustard
	1 cup sour cream
1 8¾-ounce can pineapple tidbits, drained	1½ teaspoons salt
	½ teaspoon paprika
¼ cup chopped pimientos	3 medium cantaloupes, cut in halves

Cook macaroni as directed on package. Drain. Cool. Mix together macaroni, sausage slices, pineapple tidbits, pimientos, and celery. Combine mustard, sour cream, salt and paprika; toss with macaroni mixture; chill. Scoop seeds from cantaloupes. Fill with macaroni salad. Garnish with mint sprigs, if desired. Serves 6.

MONEY-SAVER PASTA DISHES

While pasta is one of America's most popular dishes, it also is one of the most economical foods available whether for a main dish or side dish.

Virtually every one of the recipes in this chapter provides a serving for under $1.00 per person. Many are under 50¢ per serving and some are even less than 25¢ per serving. The actual cost changes with seasonal price variations in fresh produce and meat, of course, and in regional price variations where some products may not be as readily available as in other regions. Inflation over the years will affect recipe ingredients just as easily as it affects the price of cars, houses, clothing, etc. Canned or frozen vegetables and meat and other ingredients bought at sale prices and put away at home can mean additional savings to you.

These are mostly main dish recipes made with macaroni, spaghetti or egg noodles. They have been selected for their attractive appearance, taste appeal and food value as well as economy. Count on these low-priced, highly nutritive recipes when you plan your food budget.

This entire cookbook contains many other recipes which are money savers, too. This chapter merely focuses your attention on a few good examples.

Pasta products always provide a nourishment bonus at very low cost. If you would like to learn more about the subject, you can turn to the Appendix at the back of the book where you will find a study of the nutritive value of pasta.

INSIDE-OUT RAVIOLI

8 ounces (2 cups) shell or elbow macaroni
1 pound ground beef
½ cup chopped onion
1 clove garlic, minced
1 10-ounce package frozen chopped spinach
1 16-ounce jar prepared spaghetti sauce with mushrooms

1 8-ounce can tomato sauce
1 6-ounce can tomato paste
½ teaspoon salt
1 teaspoon sugar
Dash pepper
1 cup shredded process American cheese
½ cup soft bread crumbs
2 well beaten eggs

Brown ground beef, onion, garlic in large skillet. Drain excess fat. Cook spinach as directed on package. Drain, but reserve liquid and add water to make 1 cup. To meat mixture add spinach liquid, spaghetti sauce, tomato sauce, tomato paste, salt, sugar and pepper. Simmer 10 minutes. Meanwhile, cook macaroni as directed on package. Drain. Combine spinach with the macaroni, cheese, bread crumbs, eggs; spread in a 13x9x2-inch baking dish. Top with meat sauce. Bake at 350° for 30 minutes. Let stand 10 minutes. Serves 8.

SPAGHETTI WITH CHICKEN CACCIATORE

8 ounces spaghetti
2½-pound broiler-fryer chicken, cut in serving pieces
3 tablespoons salad oil

3 8-ounce cans tomato sauce
1 6-ounce can tomato paste

½ cup chopped green
   pepper
½ cup chopped onion
1 garlic clove, minced
1 teaspoon salt

¼ teaspoon pepper
¼ teaspoon orégano
½ pound fresh mushrooms,
   sliced

In a large skillet brown chicken in oil. Remove chicken
and drain off drippings. Combine tomato sauce, tomato
paste, green pepper, onion, garlic, salt, pepper and orégano
in skillet; bring to a boil, stirring occasionally. Add
chicken and cook covered 30 minutes. Add mushrooms
and cook 15 minutes longer. Meanwhile, cook spaghetti
as directed on package. Drain. Serve chicken and sauce
over hot cooked spaghetti. Serves 4.

EGG NOODLES WITH MADCAP SAUCE

8 ounces (4 cups) medium
   egg noodles
1½ teaspoons salad oil
1 small onion, sliced
1 garlic clove, finely
   chopped
¾ pound ground beef

1 8-ounce can tomato
   sauce
1 1-pound can tomatoes
1 teaspoon salt
⅛ teaspoon pepper
¼ teaspoon orégano

Heat oil over medium heat; add onion, garlic and beef and
cook until beef is browned. Add tomato sauce, tomatoes,
salt, pepper and orégano and cook 15 minutes, stirring
occasionally. Meanwhile, cook noodles as directed on
package. Drain. Serve sauce over noodles. Serves 4.

HAM-A-RONI

2 cups jumbo or large
   elbow macaroni
¼ cup chopped onion
3 tablespoons margarine
1 8-ounce can tomato sauce
1 tablespoon chili sauce
1 teaspoon salt

½ teaspoon dry mustard
1 cup water
4 slices baked ham
8 broccoli spears, cooked
   Grated Parmesan cheese
   (optional)

Cook macaroni as directed on package. Meanwhile, sauté onion in 1 tablespoon of the margarine about 5 minutes. Then add tomato sauce, chili sauce, salt, mustard and water; stir. Bring to a boil and simmer for 2 minutes. Turn macaroni into a buttered baking dish (12x8 inches) or 2-quart casserole. Place ham slices on macaroni; top ham with broccoli spears. Pour sauce mixture over all. Dot broccoli with remaining 2 tablespoons margarine. Bake in 350° oven 35 minutes. Sprinkle grated Parmesan cheese over top, if desired. Serves 4.

EGG 'N' NOODLE SALAD

2 ounces (1 cup) egg noodles	6 hard-cooked eggs, coarsely chopped
2 cups diced unpared apple (1 large apple)	1 teaspoon grated onion
1 cup grated carrots	1 cup cooked salad dressing
½ cup chopped sweet pickles	1 teaspoon salt

Cook noodles as directed on package. Drain. Cool. Mix lightly with other ingredients; chill. Serves 6.

FLORENTINE TUNA NOODLE CASSEROLE

8 ounces (4 cups) fine egg noodles	Basic White Sauce (see next page)
1 10-ounce package frozen chopped spinach, cooked and drained	2 ounces process Gruyère cheese, grated
2 6½- or 7-ounce cans tuna, drained	Paprika

Cook noodles as directed on package. Drain. Layer noodles, spinach and tuna in 2½-quart casserole. Pour white sauce on top. Sprinkle with cheese and paprika. Bake in 375° oven 20 minutes, or until bubbling. Serves 4 or 5.

A Basic White Sauce: In a saucepan, sauté 1 chopped onion in ⅓ cup margarine until almost tender. Reduce heat. Blend in ⅓ cup flour, 1 chicken bouillon cube, ¾ teaspoon salt, ¼ teaspoon white pepper and ⅛ teaspoon nutmeg. Gradually add 2 cups milk; stir in 1¼ cups water. Cook, stirring constantly, until sauce boils 1 minute.

DEVILED SPAGHETTI

1 pound spaghetti	2 cups milk
1 tablespoon chopped onion	1 2¾-ounce can deviled ham
1 tablespoon chopped green pepper	¼ teaspoon Worcestershire
3 tablespoons margarine	¾ cup grated American cheese
3 tablespoons flour	

Cook spaghetti as directed on package. Drain. Sauté onion and green pepper in margarine; then blend in the flour. Add milk gradually to make sauce. Cook until slightly thickened. Then blend in the deviled ham and Worcestershire. Arrange spaghetti in a 3-quart casserole or baking dish. Top with grated cheese and pour sauce over all. Bake in 375° oven, uncovered, 20 minutes. Serves 6 to 8.

TUNA NOODLE HOT DISH

8 ounces (4 cups) medium egg noodles	⅛ teaspoon pepper
1 small onion, chopped	3 cups milk
½ cup sliced celery	2 6½- or 7-ounce cans tuna, drained
⅓ cup margarine	1 teaspoon Worcestershire
⅓ cup flour	1 teaspoon lemon juice
1½ teaspoons salt	Paprika
½ teaspoon thyme	

Cook noodles as directed on package. Drain. In a saucepan, cook onion and celery in margarine until crisp-tender. Quickly mix in flour, salt, thyme and pepper. Gradually add milk; cook, stirring constantly, until sauce boils 1 minute. Add tuna, Worcestershire and lemon juice. Combine with noodles in 2-quart casserole. Sprinkle with paprika. Bake in 350° oven 20 minutes. Serves 4.

MACARONI AND CHEESE SALAD

1 pound (4 cups) elbow macaroni	2 teaspoons salt
	2 teaspoons grated onion
2 cups (8 ounces) shredded Cheddar cheese	1½ cups mayonnaise
	2 teaspoons vinegar
1 cup chopped green pepper	1½ teaspoons dry mustard
	Dash of pepper
1 cup chopped celery	

Cook macaroni as directed on package. Drain. Cool. Toss macaroni with other ingredients; chill. Serves 8.

MAIN DISH NOODLE PUDDING

12 ounces (6 cups) fine egg noodles	¼ teaspoon nutmeg
	1 12-ounce can luncheon meat, finely diced
2 tablespoons salad oil	
1¼ cups chopped onion	4 eggs
½ cup chopped parsley	2 cups reliquefied non-fat dry milk crystals
1½ teaspoons salt	
¼ teaspoon freshly ground black pepper	⅓ cup grated Parmesan cheese

Cook noodles as directed on package. Drain. Heat oil in a large skillet over medium heat; add onion and sauté until golden. Stir in parsley and cook just until wilted. Remove skillet from heat; stir in salt, pepper, nutmeg and meat. In buttered 2½-quart casserole, alternate 3 layers of noodles with 3 layers of meat mixture, beginning with noodles and ending with meat.

Beat eggs, milk and cheese together in bowl; pour over mixture in casserole. Bake covered in 350° oven 35 minutes; uncover and bake 20 minutes more, or until a knife inserted in center comes out clean. Serves 6.

SPAGHETTI WITH CHICKEN-LIVER SAUCE

1 pound spaghetti	1 1-pound can plum
4 tablespoons margarine	tomatoes
1 cup chopped onion	1 6-ounce can tomato
2 garlic cloves, crushed	paste
⅓ cup chopped parsley	2 beef bouillon cubes
1 teaspoon salt	dissolved in 1½ cups
Dash of pepper	boiling water
1½ teaspoons orégano	1 pound chicken livers,
¼ teaspoon thyme	sliced
1 teaspoon Worcestershire	½ cup grated Parmesan
	cheese

Melt 2 tablespoons of the margarine in a large skillet over medium heat; add onion and garlic and sauté until tender. Set 1 tablespoon of the parsley aside for garnish; add remaining parsley, salt, other seasonings, tomatoes, tomato paste and bouillon to onion mixture. Cover and cook over low heat 30 minutes, stirring occasionally.

Sauté livers in remaining 2 tablespoons margarine over low heat for 5 minutes; add to sauce. Simmer sauce, uncovered, about 5 minutes more, stirring occasionally.

Meanwhile, cook spaghetti as directed on package. Drain. Blend half of cheese into chicken-liver sauce. Serve with spaghetti sprinkled with reserved cheese and parsley. Serves 6.

SPAGHETTI WITH "RED HOT" SAUCE

8 ounces spaghetti	1 1-pound can tomatoes
3 tablespoons margarine	1 6-ounce can tomato paste
½ cup chopped onion	⅛ to ¼ teaspoon crushed red
1 garlic clove, minced	pepper
1 pound frankfurters, sliced	1 teaspoon salt
diagonally	¼ teaspoon orégano
3 tablespoons chopped	
parsley	

Melt margarine in a 10-inch skillet and add onion, garlic and frankfurters; cook over medium heat until frankfurters are browned. Add parsley, undrained tomatoes, tomato paste, red pepper, salt and orégano; mix well and cook, uncovered, over medium heat 20 minutes. Cover and continue cooking 20 minutes longer.

Meanwhile, cook spaghetti as directed on package. Drain. Serve sauce over hot cooked spaghetti. Serves 4 to 6.

SPAGHETTI WITH SALMON SAUCE

- 1 pound spaghetti
- 3 tablespoons chopped onion
- ¾ cup margarine
- 2 8-ounce bottles clam juice
- ½ cup chopped parsley
- ½ teaspoon salt
- ½ teaspoon dillweed
- ¼ teaspoon pepper
- 3 tablespoons lemon juice
- 2 1-pound cans salmon, drained and boned

Cook spaghetti as directed on package. Drain. Meanwhile, in a saucepan cook onion in margarine until tender. Stir in clam juice, parsley, salt, dillweed, pepper and lemon juice; simmer 2 minutes. Add small chunks of salmon and heat thoroughly. Serve over spaghetti. Serves 8.

NOODLE SKILLET SCRAMBLE

- 8 ounces (4 cups) wide egg noodles
- 1 8-ounce can tomato sauce with tomato bits
- ½ cup beef bouillon or broth
- 2 teaspoons salt
- ¼ teaspoon coarse black pepper
- 1½ teaspoons orégano
- ¼ teaspoon thyme
- ¼ teaspoon Worcestershire
- 3 tablespoons salad oil
- 1 pound ground beef chuck
- 1¼ cups chopped onions
- 1 garlic clove, crushed
- 1 medium green pepper, diced
- 2 cups sliced celery
- ½ cup chopped parsley

Blend tomato sauce, bouillon and seasonings in a bowl; set aside. Heat oil in a large skillet over medium heat; add beef and stir constantly until browned. Remove beef with slotted spoon and set aside. Sauté onions, garlic, green pepper and celery in drippings in skillet until crisp-tender. Cover skillet and cook 6 to 8 minutes more over low heat, stirring occasionally. Stir in parsley.

Meanwhile, cook noodles as directed on package. Drain. Add reserved beef, tomato-sauce mixture and hot cooked noodles to vegetables in skillet; toss lightly until combined. Cook just until hot. Serves 4.

GAUCHO SKILLET SUPPER

8 ounces (2 cups) macaroni twirls
1 tablespoon salad oil
6 frankfurters, sliced diagonally
½ cup chopped onion
½ cup diced green pepper
2 8-ounce cans tomato sauce with cheese
1 1-pound can kidney beans
½ cup water
2 teaspoons chili powder
1 teaspoon salt
¼ teaspoon Tabasco

Cook macaroni as directed on package. Drain. Meanwhile, in a large skillet, heat oil and brown frankfurter slices, onion and green pepper. Add macaroni and remaining ingredients. Simmer, stirring occasionally, 15 to 20 minutes. Serves 6.

CHILETTI AND FRANKS

8 ounces spaghetti
1½ teaspoons salad oil
1 medium onion, coarsely chopped
1 garlic clove, minced
4 frankfurters, cut in quarters lengthwise
1 8-ounce can tomato sauce
1 1-pound can tomatoes
½ teaspoon salt
½ teaspoon chili powder

Cook spaghetti as directed on package. Drain. Meanwhile, heat oil; add onion and garlic and sauté lightly. Add frankfurters and cook until browned. Add tomato sauce, tomatoes, salt and chili powder; mix well. Heat to boiling point and simmer 20 minutes. Serve over spaghetti. Serves 4.

SOUFFLE OF EGG NOODLES

4 ounces (2 cups) fine egg noodles
¼ cup margarine
⅓ cup chopped onion
3 tablespoons flour
1 teaspoon salt
⅛ teaspoon Tabasco
2 cups milk

2 teaspoons prepared mustard
½ cup grated Parmesan cheese
3 eggs, separated
¼ cup chopped stuffed olives
⅛ teaspoon cream of tartar

Cook noodles as directed on package. Drain. Meanwhile, melt margarine in saucepan over medium heat; add onion and sauté until golden. Stir in flour, salt and Tabasco; gradually add milk. Bring mixture to a boil, stirring constantly; cook 1 minute. Remove saucepan from heat; stir in mustard and cheese. Beat egg yolks in large bowl until frothy. Gradually stir hot sauce into egg-yolk mixture. Combine sauce mixture with noodles and olives in large bowl. Beat egg whites with cream of tartar until soft peaks form. Turn mixture into buttered 1½-quart soufflé dish. Set dish in pan of hot water. Bake in 375° oven 1 hour, or until set. Remove dish from water and garnish soufflé with parsley sprigs and olive slices if desired. Serves 4.

SPAGHETTI WITH EXTENDER MEAT SAUCE

12 ounces spaghetti
1 pound ground beef
1 onion, chopped
2 tablespoons salad oil
1 teaspoon salt

½ teaspoon orégano
½ teaspoon thyme
¼ teaspoon pepper
2 8-ounce cans tomato sauce with mushrooms

Sauté ground beef and onion in oil with salt, orégano, thyme and pepper. Pour off excess fat. Add tomato sauce. Cook slowly for 15 minutes. Meanwhile, cook spaghetti as directed on package. Drain. Pour sauce over hot spaghetti. Serves 6 to 8.

MEATY MACARONI AND CHEESE

8 ounces (2 cups) short-cut
  elbow macaroni
1 tablespoon margarine
1 pound ground beef chuck
½ cup chopped onion
½ cup sliced celery

1 15-ounce can tomato
  sauce with tomato bits
1 teaspoon salt
¼ teaspoon pepper
1 cup shredded Cheddar
  cheese

Cook macaroni as directed on package. Drain. Melt margarine in a large skillet; brown beef, onion and celery lightly. Pour off excess fat. Stir in tomato sauce, salt and pepper. Combine with macaroni and pour into 2-quart casserole. Top with shredded cheese. Bake in 350° oven for 25 minutes. Serves 5 or 6.

STUFFED FLANK STEAK

2 ounces (1 cup) medium
  egg noodles
3 cups beef bouillon
2 tablespoons minced
  onion

¼ cup finely sliced celery
½ teaspoon basil
1½ to 2-pound flank steak
  Salt and pepper
3 tablespoons margarine

Bring bouillon to a boil. Add noodles and boil rapidly 2 minutes, stirring constantly. Drain, reserving bouillon for cooking steak. Add onion, celery and basil to noodles and mix well. Season steak with salt and pepper. Arrange noodle mixture over steak and roll it up. Hold edges together with metal skewers. Tie securely with string and then remove skewers. Heat margarine in Dutch oven. Add steak and brown on all sides. Place rack under steak. Add reserved bouillon. Cover, and bake in 350° oven about 2 hours. Add hot water, if necessary. To serve, slice diagonally. Serves 6.

FRANKFURTER AND NOODLE CASSEROLE

8 ounces (4 cups) wide egg noodles	2 tablespoons Worcestershire
1 pound frankfurters	1 10-ounce can condensed tomato soup
1 medium onion, chopped	½ cup water
2 tablespoons margarine	½ teaspoon salt
¼ pound Cheddar cheese, shredded	

Cook noodles as directed on package. Drain. Cut frankfurters into long thin strips, lengthwise, and brown with the onion in the margarine. Add remaining ingredients and cook, stirring frequently, until cheese melts. Combine with noodles and place in a buttered casserole. Bake in 400° oven 25 minutes. Serves 6 to 8.

MACARONI-TOMATO AU GRATIN

3 cups large elbow macaroni	½ pound Cheddar cheese, grated
1 1-pound can whole tomatoes	

Cook macaroni as directed on package. Drain. Meanwhile, heat tomatoes to boiling. Lift tomatoes from their juice and add, with cheese, immediately to drained macaroni. Toss until cheese is melted, adding enough of the hot tomato juice to achieve desired moistness. Serves 6.

NOODLES NATASHA

6 ounces (3 cups) wide egg   2 tablespoons salad
    noodles   seasoning
¾ cup sour cream

Cook noodles as directed on package. Drain. Stir in sour cream and salad seasoning; toss lightly. Serves 4.

NOODLE FRITTERS

12 ounces (6 cups) fine egg   1 teaspoon salt
    noodles   ¼ teaspoon pepper
½ cup margarine   1 grated onion (optional)
4 eggs   Shortening for frying
3 tablespoons milk

Cook noodles as directed on package; drain. Melt margarine and mix with noodles. Beat eggs, milk, salt, pepper and onion together; pour over noodles and mix thoroughly. Now heat a griddle or large skillet; brush with a light coating of shortening (just as you do for frying pancakes) and drop noodle mixture from a tablespoon. Make the fritters about 3 inches in diameter. Fry over moderate heat until brown and crisp on one side. Turn with pancake turner, fry the second side. Serves 8. Delightful with any meal!

PASTA ALFRESCO

We Americans are a mobile people—and this goes for our dining habits. We move from house to backyard or patio, we go on picnics in the woods, we lay down a blanket and spread out a feast at the beach. Pasta is often a part of this mobility. It's easy food to take along—in wide-mouth vacuum jars, in salad crispers with keep-cold compartments, and in all sorts of insulated boxes and bags made for keeping food hot or cold when you're on the go. Lacking these, you can always wrap a hot or cold pasta dish in aluminum foil and insulate it with several thicknesses of newspaper. It's a trick that works even on long trips.

Keeping in mind that distance from home, travel time and on-site dining facilities must guide your plans, here are some recipes suitable for outdoor dining. Remember, however, that backyard meals can and should have the same variety and excitement as indoor dining. Serve versatile pasta casseroles, side dishes and salads to spark your family's alfresco appetites.

PICNIC SPAGHETTI

1 pound spaghetti
¼ cup diced green pepper
2 tablespoons chopped
    onion
2 tablespoons salad oil
2 pounds frankfurters, cut
    into 1-inch slices

2 8-ounce cans tomato
    sauce
¼ teaspoon orégano
¼ teaspoon Tabasco

Cook spaghetti as directed on package. Drain. Meanwhile, sauté green pepper and onion in oil until crisp-tender. Add frankfurters and brown lightly. Stir in remaining ingredients; simmer uncovered 5 minutes. Toss lightly with spaghetti and turn into heated 1-gallon wide-mouth vacuum jug. Serves 6 to 8.

DEVILED MACARONI SALAD

1½ pounds (6 cups) elbow
    macaroni
1 cup finely diced green
    pepper
1 cup diced celery
⅓ cup chopped pimiento
3 tablespoons minced
    onion
1½ cups mayonnaise

1 cup sour cream
3 tablespoons prepared
    spicy brown mustard
3 to 4 teaspoons salt
1½ teaspoons caraway seed
¼ teaspoon pepper
    Deviled Eggs (below)
    Parsley

Cook macaroni as directed on package. Drain. Cool. Combine with remaining ingredients except deviled eggs and parsley; toss lightly and chill. Serve with deviled eggs; garnish with parsley. Serves 12.

Deviled eggs: Halve 12 hard-cooked eggs. Remove and sieve yolks. Blend yolks with 3 tablespoons mayonnaise, 1 tablespoon prepared mustard, ½ teaspoon Tabasco and ¼ teaspoon salt. Fill whites with yolk mixture and garnish with parsley and pimiento, if desired. Makes 24 halves.

HOLIDAY NOODLES AND HAMBURGERS

8 ounces (4 cups) wide egg noodles	2 cups diced green peppers
Holiday Hamburgers (below)	½ cup finely chopped green onions
¼ cup butter	¼ cup diced pimientos
	Salt and pepper

First prepare holiday hamburgers. Then melt butter in a large skillet over medium heat; add green peppers, green onions and sauté 6 to 8 minutes, until tender. Stir in pimientos. Cook noodles as directed on package. Drain. Toss hot noodles with sautéed vegetable mixture; season to taste with salt and pepper. Turn into serving dish and top with holiday hamburgers.

Holiday Hamburgers: Beat 1 egg, 1 tablespoon water, 2 teaspoons prepared mustard, 1 teaspoon salt and ⅛ teaspoon pepper in large bowl. Add 1 pound ground beef chuck, ¼ cup grated Parmesan cheese, ¼ cup finely chopped green onions, ¼ cup finely chopped parsley; toss all ingredients lightly until combined. Shape into 4 patties; grill or broil on rack 3 to 4 inches from source of heat until hamburgers are of desired doneness, 8 to 12 minutes. Turn hamburgers once. (Hamburgers may be cooked in frying pan, if desired.) Makes 4.

BARBECUED SPAGHETTI PEPPERS

1 pound spaghetti	½ teaspoon pepper
Barbecue Sauce (see next page)	¼ cup water
	½ cup chopped onion
1½ pounds ground beef	Butter
1½ teaspoons salt	6 green peppers

Prepare barbecue sauce (this may be prepared ahead and refrigerated). Toss beef, salt, pepper, water and onion together lightly with a fork. Divide and form into 6 thick patties, handling as little as possible. Arrange patties on cold broiler pan or an outdoor grill. Brush with barbecue sauce. Broil 3 inches from heat, turning once. Brush again with sauce. Do not flatten. Allow 5 to 8 minutes of cooking time per side.

Meanwhile, cook spaghetti as directed on package. Drain. Dot with butter. Wash peppers and cut in half lengthwise. Remove seeds, stems and ribs. Cook in boiling water 4 to 5 minutes, until just fork tender. Fill with spaghetti. Place on hot platter with meat patties. Serve any remaining sauce on the side. Serves 6.

Barbecue Sauce:

½ cup chopped onion
1 garlic clove, minced
1 7-ounce can sliced mushrooms (reserve liquid)
2 tablespoons butter
Mushroom liquid and water to make ½ cup
3 8-ounce cans tomato sauce

1 cup diced green pepper
½ teaspoon dry mustard
2 tablespoons brown sugar
1 teaspoon chili powder
1 teaspoon barbecue spice
¾ teaspoon salt
¼ teaspoon Tabasco
½ cup grated Cheddar cheese

Sauté onion, garlic and mushrooms in butter until onion is transparent. Add remaining ingredients except cheese, and simmer 20 minutes. Add cheese and stir until it is melted.

Here is a listing of additional recipes in this book adaptable to picnics and outdoors dining:

AS YOU LIKE IT SPAGHETTI AND MEAT BALLS　　14
PARTY MACARONI CHILI　　17
RIPPLETS AND SAUERBRATEN　　26
SAM'S HEARTY BEEF CASSEROLE　　32
MOSTACCIOLI WITH RICH TOMATO BEEF SAUCE　　37

BARBECUED RIBS WITH SPAGHETTI	41
DIVINE TURKEY MEDLEY	49
CHICKEN MARENGO WITH NOODLES	54
RIPPLETS WITH THREE CHEESES	59
CHEDDAR NOODLE CASSEROLE	61
TUNA TETRAZZINI	68
DIPSY NOODLES	79
MACARONI AND TUNA GARDEN SALAD	85
TUNA SUPPER SALAD	86
SHELL-CHICKEN SALAD	87
PICNIC MACARONI SALAD	88
RANCHO MACARONI SALAD	89
LASAGNE ROLLS WITH MEAT SAUCE	96
PARMA NOODLES	106
MACARONI CASSEROLE ITALIANO	110
NOODLE MINESTRONE	118
MEAT BALL SOUP WITH RINGS	120
SOUR CREAM NOODLE BAKE	130
SEACOAST SALAD	131
ITALIAN-STYLE SHORT RIBS	135
LASAGNE-STYLE NOODLE CASSEROLE	136
HAM-A-RONI	160
EGG 'N' NOODLE SALAD	161
TUNA NOODLE HOT DISH	162
GAUCHO SKILLET SUPPER	166
MEATY MACARONI AND CHEESE	168
STUFFED FLANK STEAK	168

PROFITABLE PASTA DINNERS
FOR CHURCH GROUPS
AND CLUBS

Many churches and clubs boost their treasuries or raise money for special activities by serving luncheons and dinners. Pasta dishes are a good choice for fund-raising events because pasta products have wide appeal, are relatively low in cost, simple to prepare, and give you a chance to make an excellent profit.

Some organizations have facilities and equipment for preparing food for large numbers; the recipes in this chapter are intended for such organizations. But even if your facilities are quite limited, you can still have a fund-raising meal by asking a number of members to bring hot pasta casseroles or main-dish salads to serve 10 to 12. Recipes in the buffet chapter and many others in this book "travel" and hold well for meals of this type. Members who provide the food can be reimbursed for the ingredients or receive free tickets, depending on the policy you establish.

The food you serve need not be elaborate, as everyone enjoys eating out when the price is right and the proceeds go to a worthwhile cause. Feature an Italian gala and the menu can be as simple as Spaghetti and Meat Balls, Tossed Green Salad, Crusty French Bread and Fresh

Whole Fruit with Cookies. Or you may prefer to get a
little fancier and serve Veal Birds Parmigiano, Green
Beans, Cream-Style Corn, Combination Salad with Rus-
sian Dressing, Assorted Relishes, Crescent Rolls and
Strawberry Bavarian Cream. It is better, however, to start
on a modest scale and build up the array after a smooth
operating pattern has been established.

Organizing the work and spreading the responsibility
is the secret of any large undertaking. Appoint a commit-
tee to work with you and be sure to delegate authority.
Consider the purpose—social, money raising, or both—and
plan accordingly. Evaluate your facilities and decide how
you can best handle the serving before you choose the
menu. Type of service, menu and facilities are closely
related. One high spot in the meal—whether a special-dish
main course, a salad, or a dessert—makes for success.

To decide what you will charge, consider all costs.
Make up your marketing list, check food prices, decora-
tions, laundry or disposables, paid help and any rental or
other overhead. Now compute the cost per person by di-
viding the sum of all your costs by the expected guests,
then add the figure you wish to make as a profit. Allow
for cancelled reservations and nonpaying guests. It is ad-
visable to add about five percent to cover any unprevent-
able loss in handling the food.

Don't overlook publicity, ticket printing and cleanup
in your plans. Once you have staged a successful event
you can always draw crowds and establish the money-
making dinner as an important source of revenue for your
organization. Good luck and good profits!

DIRECTIONS FOR COOKING LARGE QUANTITIES

1. Use correct proportion of water, salt and pasta. Use 4
   to 6 quarts rapidly boiling water and 2 tablespoons salt
   for each pound of spaghetti, macaroni or egg noodles.
   (Add 2 teaspoons salad or olive oil per pound of pasta,
   if desired. See page 7.)

2. The amount to be cooked at one time depends on the sizes of saucepots available. For best results, cook only small amounts—no more than 5 pounds—at a time. Using the recommended proportions, 5 pounds would require ½ cup plus 2 tablespoons salt and 5 to 7½ gallons water.

3. Be sure the water is boiling rapidly before adding spaghetti, macaroni or egg noodles. Add pasta gradually so that water continues to boil.

4. Read the package directions, as cooking time varies according to the size and thickness of the pasta. Start timing after all the pasta is added and water is again boiling rapidly. Do not overcook. Pasta should be tender but firm. The best way to check for doneness is to taste the pasta during the cooking process.

5. Stir occasionally and gently to keep pasta evenly distributed and moving in the boiling water so that all of it will be evenly cooked. If the pasta will be used in a casserole, reduce boiling time by one-third.

6. When macaroni product is tender, drain in colander. Do not rinse, unless product is to be used in cold salad; then rinse in cold water and drain again.

VEAL BIRDS PARMIGIANO

6 pounds thin spaghetti or vermicelli	1 quart flour
2 quarts dry bread crumbs	2 cups butter
1 cup minced onion	2 pounds mozzarella cheese, sliced
1 quart mushrooms, drained, chopped and sautéed	2 quarts prepared spaghetti sauce
8 eggs, beaten	2 cups butter, melted
4 cups beef stock or water	2 cups hot milk
1 teaspoon rosemary	2 cups grated Parmesan cheese
100 pieces boneless veal steak, ¼-inch thick and 4x2 inches (about 16 pounds)	1 tablespoon salt

Mix together bread crumbs, onion, mushrooms, eggs, 1 cup beef stock or water and rosemary. Spread on veal pieces. Roll veal; secure with food picks. Dredge veal with flour; brown in butter. Place in shallow baking pans. Cover bottom of pans with remaining beef stock or water. Bake, covered, in 350° oven until tender, about 30 minutes. Remove meat from oven; top with mozzarella cheese and cover with sauce. Bake, uncovered, 10 minutes. Cook spaghetti as directed. Drain. Combine melted butter, hot milk, Parmesan cheese and salt. Toss with spaghetti. Serve 2 veal birds on each portion of spaghetti. Serves 50.

BEEF STROGANOFF WITH NOODLES

6 pounds wide egg noodles	2½ quarts mushrooms, sliced
5 cups flour	1 quart onions, chopped
3 tablespoons salt	9 garlic cloves, minced
1 tablespoon pepper	2½ quarts beef stock or condensed beef broth
16 pounds beef round steak, cut in strips ½x2 inches	3 quarts sour cream
2 pounds butter	½ cup parsley flakes
	1 cup sherry

Combine 3 cups flour, the salt and pepper. Dredge beef strips with flour mixture; brown quickly in butter. Add mushrooms, onions and garlic; brown lightly. Add 1½ quarts of the beef stock. Simmer, covered, until meat is tender, about 1 hour.

Blend together sour cream, remaining 2 cups flour and the parsley flakes. Gradually add remaining 1 quart beef stock. Heat, stirring constantly, until mixture thickens. *Do not boil.* Add to beef mixture; stir to combine. Heat to serving temperature. Stir in sherry.

Cook noodles as directed. Drain. Serve with beef stroganoff. Serves 50.

SPAGHETTI AND MEAT BALLS

MEAT BALLS

1 half of 1-pound loaf of day-old bread	½ pound onions, chopped
8 pounds ground beef	1 teaspoon pepper
½ pound ground pork	2 tablespoons salt
1 egg	1 cup beef stock (about)

Soak bread in water, press out excess moisture, and discard water. Mix all ingredients except stock together and form into 2-ounce meatballs (#16 scoop). Place in buttered baking pan and brown. Add enough stock to half-cover the meat balls. Bake in 350° oven 30 minutes.

SPAGHETTI

3⅓ pounds Italian style spaghetti	1 gallon tomato sauce, heated

Cook spaghetti as directed. Drain. Pour hot tomato sauce over and heat well. Serve 2 meat balls on each portion of spaghetti. Serves 25 to 30.

NOTE: Part or all of the meat ball drippings may be added to the tomato sauce to make it richer, if desired.

SPAGHETTI WITH TOMATO-MEAT SAUCE

8 pounds spaghetti	2 29-ounce cans tomato purée
4 8-ounce cans sliced mushrooms	8 6-ounce cans tomato paste
1 cup shortening	1 quart hot water
5 pounds onions, chopped	12 bay leaves, crumbled
½ cup garlic chips	¼ cup sugar
15 pounds finely ground beef	2 teaspoons pepper
½ cup salt	½ teaspoon cayenne
2 6½-pound cans tomatoes	1 tablespoon orégano

Drain mushrooms, reserving liquid. Melt shortening. Add mushrooms, onions, garlic, beef and salt. Cook, stirring frequently, until beef is well browned. Add remaining ingredients, including mushroom liquid, except spaghetti. Simmer 2 hours, stirring occasionally. If sauce becomes too thick, add hot water. Skim fat from sauce before serving. Cook spaghetti as directed. Drain, and serve with sauce poured over. Serves 100.

MEATLESS ITALIAN SPAGHETTI

5 pounds spaghetti	1 6½-pound can tomatoes
2 cups cooking oil	4 bay leaves
4 teaspoons black pepper	2½ tablespoons salt
2½ cups sliced onions	½ cup sugar
1½ cups tomato paste	2 cups grated Parmesan
1 quart water	cheese

Heat oil in a heavy kettle. Add pepper and heat for 2 minutes. Add onions and cook until a delicate brown. Mix tomato paste with water and add gradually to the onions, allowing it to boil up after each addition. Add tomatoes, bay leaves and salt and simmer 45 minutes. Add sugar and cook 15 minutes longer. Cook spaghetti as directed. Drain and mix with tomato sauce. Sprinkle with cheese and serve. Serves 50.

MACARONI MILANESE

3 pounds large elbow macaroni	1 large onion, minced
2 28-ounce cans tomatoes	1½ cups flour
3 peppercorns	2 quarts beef stock
5 bay leaves	Salt and pepper
2 tablespoons sugar	4 pounds cooked ham, cubed
1½ cups butter	

Cook macaroni as directed. Drain. Place tomatoes in kettle. Add peppercorns, bay leaves and sugar, and simmer

10 minutes. Push mixture through a strainer. Melt butter, add onion, and cook until soft. Stir in flour. Add stock and tomato mixture and cook and stir until mixture boils. Season to taste. In large buttered baking pans make layers of macaroni, ham and sauce, ending with sauce. Bake in 350° oven 25 minutes, or until thoroughly heated. Serves 50.

CASSEROLE OF HAM, MACARONI AND BROCCOLI

3 pounds elbow macaroni	1½ gallons milk
3 pounds cooked ham	1 teaspoon vinegar
6 pounds broccoli	2 tablespoons grated
¾ pound butter, melted	onion
2 cups flour	4½ cups grated Cheddar
2 teaspoons salt	cheese
½ teaspoon white pepper	2 cups grated Parmesan
½ teaspoon dry mustard	cheese

Cut ham into ¾-inch cubes. Cut broccoli into 1-inch pieces. Cook broccoli in boiling salted water until slightly underdone. Drain. Melt butter. Blend in flour, salt, pepper and mustard. Add milk and cook, stirring constantly, until thickened. Stir in vinegar and onion. Add Cheddar cheese and stir until it melts.

Cook macaroni as directed. Drain. Combine with ham, broccoli and cheese sauce. Place approximately 7 ounces of the mixture in each of 50 buttered 8-ounce individual casseroles. Sprinkle 2 teaspoons grated Parmesan over top of each casserole. Bake in 375° oven until sauce is bubbly and cheese is melted, 10 to 15 minutes. Serves 50.

SAUSAGE MACARONI BAKE

4 pounds elbow macaroni	2½ pounds carrots, thinly
8 pounds bulk pork	sliced
sausage	1¼ pounds celery, diced
2 pounds butter	4 cups flour

1 cup instant minced onion	1½ gallons milk
1 cup instant minced onion	½ pound potato chips,
⅓ cup dry mustard	crushed
2 tablespoons salt	

Cook macaroni as directed. Drain. Meanwhile, break up sausage and brown in skillet. Drain well. Melt butter in a large pan. Add carrots and celery and cook about 10 minutes, or until almost tender but not brown. Blend together flour, onion, mustard and salt. Stir into vegetable mixture to form a smooth paste. Gradually add milk. Cook, stirring constantly, until thickened. Mix with macaroni and sausage until well blended. Turn into 2 lightly buttered pans (20x12x2 inches). Sprinkle tops with potato chips. Bake in 350° oven 30 minutes. Serves 48.

EASY MACARONI AND CHEESE BAKE

6 pounds small shells, elbow or rotini macaroni	1 teaspoon white pepper
6 pounds small shells, elbow or rotini macaroni	1½ gallons hot milk
1 pound butter, melted	4 pounds American cheese, shredded
2 cups enriched flour	Chives or paprika
⅓ cup seasoned salt	(optional)
⅓ cup dry mustard	

Blend together butter, flour, seasoned salt, mustard and pepper. Gradually add hot milk. Cook, stirring constantly until mixture thickens. Add cheese; stir until cheese melts.

Cook macaroni as directed. Drain. Divide macaroni into 2 pans (20x12x2 inches). Cover with sauce, about 1 gallon to each pan. Stir. Sprinkle with chives or paprika, if desired. Bake in 350° oven 30 minutes. Serves 50.

ITALIAN MOSTACCIOLI

| 6 pounds mostaccioli | 1¼ pounds onions, chopped |
| 2 cups chopped green peppers | 1½ cups bacon fat or salad oil |

1 6½-pound, plus 1
  28-ounce can tomatoes
1½ cups flour
¼ cup salt

2 tablespoons sugar
1 pound Parmesan cheese,
  grated

Cook mostaccioli as directed. Drain. Meanwhile, cook green peppers and onions in bacon fat until soft but not brown. Put tomatoes through a sieve. Add flour to vegetables and stir until smooth. Add tomatoes; cook and stir until thickened. Add salt, sugar and mostaccioli. Reheat over hot water. Serve sprinkled with grated cheese. Serves 50.

MACARONI LOAF

2½ pounds elbow macaroni
2 cups butter
2 cups flour
2 teaspoons salt
  Freshly ground pepper
1 gallon milk

6 eggs, beaten
½ teaspoon paprika
½ cup chopped pimientos
½ cup chopped parsley
12 ounces sharp Cheddar
  cheese, grated

Cook macaroni as directed. Drain. Melt butter and stir in flour, salt and pepper to taste. Add milk and cook, stirring constantly, until thickened and smooth. Add a little hot sauce to eggs; then return to remaining sauce. Continue to cook and stir for 5 minutes. Add paprika, pimientos, parsley and cheese. Remove from heat and stir until cheese is melted. Combine with macaroni. Pour into 2 pans (20x12x2 inches) and bake in 350° oven 25 minutes. Serve with tomato sauce. Serves 50.

FOUR-STAR CHICKEN CASSEROLE

12½ pounds elbow macaroni
3 pounds butter, melted
2½ pounds onions, chopped
1 pound, 12 ounces non-
  fat dry milk crystals
2¼ gallons water

12 3-pound, 2-ounce cans
  condensed cream of
  celery soup
3 gallons diced cooked
  chicken

1 gallon sliced cooked
　carrots
1 gallon cooked peas

3 quarts bread crumbs
2 tablespoons poultry
　seasoning

Cook macaroni as directed. Drain. Heat 1 pound butter.
Add onions and cook about 10 minutes. Mix dry milk and
water. Blend into cooked onions with soup, stirring until
smooth. Add chicken, carrots and peas to soup mixture.
Add macaroni. Place in buttered baking pans. Combine
bread crumbs, remaining melted butter and poultry seasoning. Sprinkle over tops of baking pans. Bake in 375°
oven about 25 minutes. Serves 100.

SHRIMP CURRY WITH SPAGHETTI

6 pounds thin spaghetti
2 pounds butter, melted
5 cups chopped onions
1 cup curry powder
1 quart flour
⅓ cup sugar
⅓ cup salt
1 tablespoon ginger

1 teaspoon pepper
1¾ gallons hot milk
½ cup lemon juice
50 hard-cooked eggs,
　chopped
12½ pounds shrimps (46 to
　50 count), cleaned,
　deveined and cooked

Combine butter, onions and curry powder. Cook until
onions are soft. Blend flour, sugar, salt, ginger and pepper
into onion mixture. Gradually stir in hot milk; add lemon
juice. Cook until thickened, stirring constantly. Stir in
eggs and shrimps. Heat to serving temperature. Meanwhile, cook spaghetti as directed. Drain. Serve with
shrimps and sauce. Serves 50.

CHEESY TUNA LOAF

3½ pounds elbow macaroni
3 pounds canned tuna,
　drained and flaked
3 quarts packed soft bread
　crumbs

1 quart stuffed olives,
　sliced
8 10¾-ounce cans
　condensed cheese
　soup (2½ quarts)

| 1 gallon milk | 3 tablespoons garlic salt |
| 18 eggs, beaten | 2 teaspoons dry mustard |

Cook macaroni as directed. Drain. Toss macaroni with tuna, bread crumbs and olives. Blend remaining ingredients together; pour over macaroni mixture. Stir gently to mix. Portion into buttered pans (20x12x2 inches). Bake in 350° oven until firm, 45 to 60 minutes. Serves 50.

SALMON AND SHELL MACARONI AU GRATIN

5 pounds shell macaroni	2 teaspoons paprika
8 pounds canned salmon	¼ cup salt
2 gallons Thin White Sauce (p. 60)	2 teaspoons pepper
1 cup grated onions	1 pound sharp cheese, grated
2 cups pimientos, cut in ¼-inch pieces	

Drain salmon; reserve liquid. Remove skin and any bones from salmon; flake. To Thin White Sauce add onions, pimientos, paprika, salt and pepper. Blend well. Meanwhile, cook macaroni as directed. Drain. Add cooked macaroni, salmon and liquid to sauce mixture. Put mixture into 2 well-buttered pans (20x12x4 inches). Top with grated cheese. Bake in 375° oven 30 minutes, or until cheese is melted and delicately browned. Serves 50.

NOTE: Substitute tuna or other canned fish for salmon, if desired.

SAVORY CRAB MEAT SALAD

2 pounds elbow macaroni	1 cup lemon juice
7½ pounds crab meat, drained and flaked	½ cup sugar
1 quart diced green peppers	3 tablespoons salt
	2 tablespoons dillweed
2 quarts sour cream	2 tablespoons dry mustard
2 cups milk	1 teaspoon pepper

Cook macaroni as directed. Drain. Cool. Toss crab meat and green peppers with macaroni. Blend remaining ingredients together. Pour over crab-meat mixture; mix lightly but thoroughly. Refrigerate until ready to serve. Serves 50.

MACARONI TOMATO SURPRISE

4 pounds salad macaroni	2 cups chopped green
16 hard-cooked eggs,	peppers
chopped	2 cups chopped green
2 quarts salad dressing	onions
½ cup lemon juice	50 fresh whole tomatoes
1 tablespoon celery seeds	50 lettuce leaves

Cook macaroni as directed. Drain. Cool. Toss with eggs. Combine salad dressing, lemon juice, celery seeds, green peppers, and onions. Pour over macaroni and eggs. Mix lightly but thoroughly. Refrigerate until ready to make up salads. Cut tomatoes into wedges, leaving wedges connected at base. Place on lettuce leaves; press out tomato sections to form cups. Fill each with salad. Garnish with deviled eggs if desired. Serves 50.

HOT GERMAN MACARONI SALAD

4 pounds elbow macaroni	1½ quarts cider vinegar
4 pounds canned	1¼ quarts mushroom liquid
mushrooms	1 quart chopped green
2¼ pounds bacon, diced	onions
1 quart sugar	1 quart chopped celery
¾ cup flour	1 quart sliced radishes
1 tablespoon salt	1 cup chopped parsley
1 teaspoon pepper	

Drain mushrooms; reserve liquid. Fry bacon with mushrooms until bacon is crisp. Do not drain. Add sugar, flour, salt and pepper to mushroom mixture. Stir to blend. Gradually stir in vinegar and mushroom liquid. Cook until thickened, stirring constantly; keep hot. Cook macaroni as directed. Drain. Mix thoroughly with hot dressing, green onions, and celery. Garnish with radishes and parsley. Serve hot. Serves 50.

DECORATING WITH PASTA

Pasta is an ideal craft medium just as it comes out of the package. Light in weight for its volume, pasta is amazingly strong and durable.

The craft projects described in this chapter give you an idea of pasta's versatility as a craft medium. Most are executed in mere minutes, utilizing rubber cement, as explained below, and spray-painted (from pressurized cans) with silver, gold or white paint.

HOW TO CEMENT

For temporary projects, rubber cement is easy and swift, but rubber cement can't be depended upon for long-term bonding. Brush a coat on the object to be decorated and allow a few minutes' drying time. (Wherever two semi-dry surfaces come in contact, they stick.) Then simply touch each piece of pasta with rubber cement and emplace it.

For semi-permanent projects, white glue from a squeeze bottle gives a reasonably durable bond but is not quite as quick sticking.

For permanent projects, like decorating a lamp shade,

it's probably a good idea to use the new very quick-setting epoxy resin, mixing only as much at a time as you can use before it hardens. This technique is somewhat slower going, but it provides the strongest bond of all.

WHAT TO MAKE

The number of decorative objects that can be hand-crafted with pasta is limited only by your creativity. Be as inventive as possible. Put your imagination into high gear. Experiment with shapes, designs and end-uses.

Combine pasta with other elements like buttons, beads and pearls when decorating small objects like matchboxes. The effect can be richly baroque. For a simple matchbox project, use various sizes of shell macaroni.

If you live far from the ocean you may be intrigued with the realism that can be achieved using shell macaroni, large shell macaroni and sea shell macaroni. Spray-paint the shells or leave them unpainted. Your friends will be amazed when you tell them they aren't real sea shells—but macaroni!

Try spraying shells—white, silver, gold—*before* gluing them in place.

Or glue everything down, wait for the adhesive to dry, then spray with white paint first. Let it dry and just touch the tips of elements with the gold or silver spray. A striking candle holder centerpiece can be handcrafted in this fashion. Glue various sizes of shell macaroni on a styrofoam ring base, spray, and insert five or six spiked candle holders down into the base.

TAKE HEED

A warning regarding spray-painting: Both gold and silver lose their sheens relatively quickly. So don't use them for painting an important gift. Do use them on objects for yourself or a family member if you don't mind a quick refurbishing with the spray occasionally. It takes only seconds, as you'll discover the first time you try it.

When spray-painting pasta never spray in a room where there's an open flame—don't let anyone light a cigarette. The danger is explosion and fire. Spray with adequate ventilation, outdoors if at all possible. Try not to breathe any of the spray vapor. It is not good for you in any amount; breathing too much of it is distinctly harmful. Children should not be allowed to spray-paint unsupervised.

Any day is a good day to decorate with pasta. It's simple, clean and quick. But it is at Christmastime that pasta craft really comes into its own.

Many families make their own Christmas tree ornaments, either gluing pasta to plain ornaments or using balls of styrofoam of various diameters. These are available at craft shops and party supply stores—or you can roll your own: Buy a chunk of the green styrofoam that variety stores sell for making flower arrangements. Cut a cube out of it. Cut off the corners of the cube and roll it under your hand on a hard surface, pressing firmly until it is round.

It's a good idea to attach a nylon (fishline) filament to the styrofoam ball for hanging before decorating it with pasta. Just make a sliding loop in the filament, slip it around a kitchen match that's had its head cut off, and pull taut. An extra half hitch or two will hold it secure. Then dip the matchstick in cement and insert it into the styrofoam ball. It will dry while you're decorating and the Christmas ornament will be ready to hang on the tree when you're done. A hint: Linear designs, perhaps combining ribbons or rickrack, running vertically and/or horizontally around the sphere may give you a more pleasing Christmas tree ornament than simply covering the ball all over with one kind of pasta.

MORE CHRISTMAS ELEGANCE

Make **Christmas garlands**, alternating elbow macaroni and cranberries (or Christmas-y beads) strung on nylon filament. They look lovely on your tree.

To make a **Christmas wreath**, glue a styrofoam ring onto a slightly wider ring of heavy cardboard. Emplace ripplet noodles and dumplings for a varied effect. Spray with green paint and "garnish" with red berries; tie a big bow on the completed wreath.

To make a **Christmas bell**, cut part of the neck off a quart plastic bottle, such as a bleach bottle. Cut off the lower half or two-thirds of the bottle too, leaving a bell shape. Decorate with macaroni shells, elbow macaroni and macaroni twirls. Use a small glass tree ornament suspended by a thread from inside for the bell's clapper. Spray the bell silver or gold and hang a big red ribbon on it.

Graceful, delicate **Christmas stars** to hang on your tree can be made by drawing a perfect five-pointed star shape on paper, then cutting individual pieces of thin spaghetti to the proper lengths. Lay them atop your drawing and glue them where the pieces cross one another; also touch each point of the star with glue to join the ends of the spaghetti at the points of the star. Hang with thread or nylon filament. Interesting spiky ornaments call for a small ball of styrofoam into which punch as many varied short lengths of spaghetti as you can—a lesson in dexterity when you near completion.

Dumplings and macaroni shells, spray-painted before they are glued in place, make interesting decorative embellishments on **Easter eggs**—certainly much more unusual and sculptural than the flat designs we are used to seeing.

The various sizes and shapes of tubular pasta—elbow macaroni, salad mac, rigatoni, etc.—are ideal for stringing. Macaroni jewelry is one use—necklaces, collars, bracelets. For ease in threading, dip the end of your string in glue.

PASTA PROJECTS YOU CAN WEAR

Pasta jewelry can also be fashioned by sticking tiny macaroni shells to plain earrings.

Try using alphabets for name pins. An ordinary safety pin fastened with fast-setting epoxy glue to a stiff cardboard or thin wood backing makes an ideal base on which to build a brooch. For a delicate diaphanous summer-and-sea effect, spray the backing bright sky blue and fasten shell macaroni in place with clear adhesive. Leave the shells unpainted. They will look as if they had just washed up on the beach. Glue two or three tiny seed pearls in among the shells for pretty surprise elements.

The logical extension of a pasta jewelry project is a pasta-decorated jewel box. Make one from any simple hinged-top box (a cigar box is perfect) and spray.

A FAMILY ENTERPRISE

A beaded screen of macaroni for a door or window is a strikingly beautiful craft project, but one that will take time—and probably more macaroni than you will estimate needing. But no harm, the next trip to the supermarket restores your dwindling supply. A macaroni curtain or screen, perhaps alternating "beads" of elbow macaroni and salad mac, and inserting a few glass beads as accents, can be a family project, each family member racing to see who can string fastest, a prize to the one who contributes the most strings by project's end. Hang each string individually from a little screw eye. Space them evenly across the door frame or window frame.

Turn a tin can into a fancy pencil holder by gluing pieces of spaghetti around it; encircle the bottom rim with pieces of rigatoni and the top rim with elbow macaroni, accenting both with shell macaroni.

Flower pot covers can be made the same way, the edges decorated with rows of tiny shell macaroni. If there's a chance your finished work will be subjected to water, however, shellac it both before and after painting. Just brush the shellac on quickly. It spreads itself evenly.

Inexpensive **picture frames** purchased at a variety store can be decorated with pasta and spray-painted to look far more expensive.

The reward for you as a craftsman when decorating with pasta is the look on people's faces when they discover the medium you have used in making all these beautiful objects—is pasta!

APPENDIX

A PASTA LOVER'S PRIMER

As in any other industry, pasta manufacturers have their own special words and terms. Here are the basic ones they use.

Pasta—the all-inclusive Italian word for all macaroni foods—macaroni, spaghetti, egg noodles, specialties—in their more than 300 different shapes.

Durum—an amber-colored premium grade of spring wheat used primarily in the making of quality macaroni, spaghetti and egg noodles. Durum wheat has a flint-like endosperm and is the hardest known variety of wheat. Durums have a higher level of protein than almost all varieties of other wheat. The Wheat Flour Institute says, "Careful research has shown that durum wheat, and durum wheat alone, has all the qualities to produce the finest macaroni."

Semolina—a coarse granulation of the durum wheat endosperm; by Federal definition, made by grinding and bolting durum wheat, separating bran and germ to produce a granular product of not more than 3 percent flour. Semolina is the most costly form of durum wheat and produces the finest quality possible in pasta products. All Skinner macaroni and spaghetti products are made from 100% semolina.

Durum Flour—finely ground durum wheat. Generally used for making noodles.

Macaroni—hollow tubes of various sizes, diameters and lengths, made by extruding a dough mixture (such as semolina and water) through dies in which a center pin creates the hole in the macaroni.

Spaghetti—made the same as macaroni except that the shape is rod-like, solid and generally of smaller diameter.

Noodles—strips, usually flat, rolled in sheets and cut into ribbons or extruded and cut in ribbons. By Federal definition, noodle dough must contain a minimum of 5.5 percent egg solids.

Al dente—Italian, meaning "to the tooth;" firm and chewy and cooked through, so there is no starchy flavor. Test by pressing the cooked product with a fork against the side of a pan, or better still, by actually biting and tasting.

To aficionados, *al dente* may mean that the product has a tiny, hard, still uncooked core.

GLOSSARY OF PASTA SHAPES

As you glanced through the recipes, you may have found some calling for unfamiliar pasta products, pasta that may be familiar to you by another name. Some manufacturers label their products with the traditional Italian names, others call them by their Americanized names, while still others give them imaginative new names. There are more than 300 different kinds of pasta, by name. No wonder it gets confusing!

The illustrations in this glossary cover the most popular pasta shapes and will help you find the pasta product called for in any recipe in this book or suggest a size and shape if you wish to substitute.

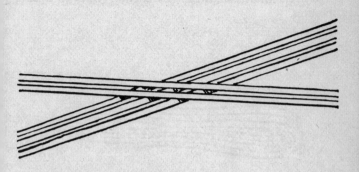

Italian Style Spaghetti—Extra long (about 16½″). Great for twirling and eating with gusto. Like Long Spaghetti, the strands are of a medium diameter.

Thin Italian Style Spaghetti—Also extra long (about 16½″), but the strands are smaller in diameter than Italian Style Spaghetti. (See illustration above.)

Long Spaghetti—The strands are the same diameter as Italian Style Spaghetti, but shorter (8¼″ long).

Thin Spaghetti—The strands are the same diameter as Thin Italian Style Spaghetti, but only 8¼″ long; also called *Spaghettini*.

Quick Cook Vermicelli—Extra thin 8¼″-long strands. The extra thin strands shorten cooking time to 2 or 3 minutes.

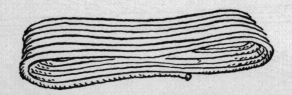

Twisted Vermicelli—Long strands of Vermicelli which have been folded or twisted; also called *Coil Capellini* and *Vermicelli Clusters.*

Ready Cut Spaghetti—Thin, short, curved rods with a fine hole in them. Use with sauce, in casseroles or in loaves.

Fine Egg Noodles—Thin pieces (3/32″ wide) used in soups and casseroles; also called *Narrow Egg Noodles.*

Medium Egg Noodles—A little wider (¼″) and used in a great variety of appetizing pasta dishes.

Wide Egg Noodles—The widest noodle (½″) with the same uses as other egg noodles; also called *Broad Egg Noodles* or *Extra Wide Egg Noodles*.

Ripplet Egg Noodles—Small pieces (⅜″ wide) with an interesting ripple or curl.

Frozen Egg Noodles—Medium in width and thicker than dry egg noodles; the closest to "homemade."

Short Cut Elbow Macaroni—Smallest in diameter of the elbow macaroni sizes; cut to short ½"-to-¾" lengths.

Large Elbow Macaroni—Larger diameter pieces cut in short ½"-to-¾" lengths.

Jumbo Elbow Macaroni—The largest diameter and length (¾" to 1¼") of elbow macaroni.

Shell Macaroni—Macaroni shaped like a shell used especially with sea food and in salads.

Large Shell Macaroni—Medium-size shells.

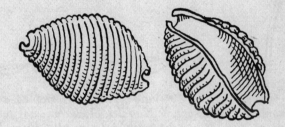

Sea Shell Macaroni—Large-size shells.

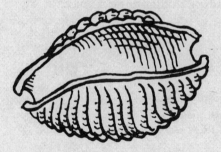

Colossus Shells—Largest of the shell macaroni family, an ideal pasta for stuffing.

Salad Mac—Very short 3/16"-to-¼" lengths; also called *Ditalini*, "little thimbles."

Lasagne—Wide, 10″-long strips with rippled edges, sometimes called *Lasagne Noodles*. However, lasagne contains no eggs; it merely resembles a noodle shape. Most often used in baked dishes with ricotta and mozzarella cheese and a rich tomato-meat sauce.

Macaroni Twirls—Spiral shape used in casseroles, side dishes and salads, as in Gaucho Skillet Supper, page 166; also called *Corkscrews*, *Rotelle* or *Rotini*.

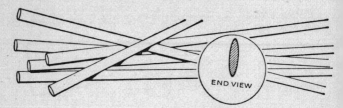

Linguini—A member of the spaghetti family; narrow oval rods. A sort of flattened spaghetti.

Alphabets—Miniature pasta in the shape of letters and numerals favored by children but enjoyed by everyone in soups.

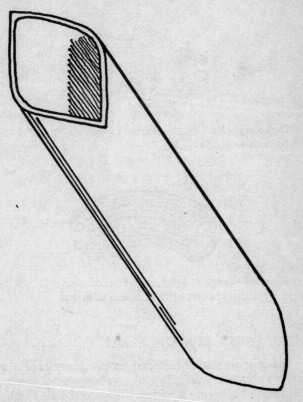

Manicotti—meaning small "muff," but actually giant tubes with the ends cut diagonally. Always stuffed with cheese, meat or a mixture of sea food. Length: 5¼".

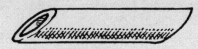

Mostaccioli—Short 1½"-to-2" lengths of medium diameter with diagonally-cut ends; also called *Penne*. Used like other macaroni cuts, as in Mostaccioli Beef Pie, page 28.

Dumplings—Flat pieces with rippled edges, used especially with stewed chicken.

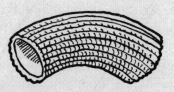

Rigatoni—Large ridged or grooved tubes (¾" to 1¾" long), usually stuffed or used in baked dishes.

HOW PASTA IS MADE

All pasta is made by mixing proper amounts of granulated wheat and water. But to create the very best pasta requires a background of knowledge and skill combined with high-quality ingredients and automated machines.

Top-quality pasta is made from a special variety of wheat called durum—an extremely hard, spring wheat grown chiefly in a 19-county area of North Dakota known as the "durum triangle." Careful research has shown that durum wheat, and durum wheat alone, has all the qualities to produce the finest pasta.

Durum wheat was brought to the U. S. from Russia earlier, but it was not grown successfully here until about 1900. Its use in macaroni products multiplied rapidly when the climate and soil of northeastern North Dakota were found to be ideal for growing durum. This premium-priced wheat is milled with special equipment either into a coarse middling product called "semolina" or into flour. Semolina is especially suited for use in all forms of pasta because the quality of the gluten in semolina tends to prevent stretching and breakage during drying, packaging and cooking. It also has a better tolerance against overcooking. Skinner makes its macaroni and spaghetti products 100% from durum wheat semolina.

Pasta made from other hard wheat types, or made from a combination of other hard wheat and durum, to save money, produces when cooked a lower quality food in appearance, flavor and texture. This sacrifice in quality usually saves only a fraction of a penny in the cost per serving. Because Skinner uses only durum wheat in the manufacture of all of its products, Skinner pasta has a lovely golden-amber color, pleasant nutty flavor and firm texture when cooked. The premium ingredients in Skinner products, and the manufacturing skills developed over almost seven decades, insure that you are getting the finest pasta available.

Modern macaroni plants are completely automated. A pneumatic unloading system transfers the semolina to bulk storage bins and another transfers it to press bins for mixing with water. The dough is kneaded, then forced through dies, which are heavy metal discs with holes. The size and shape of the holes determine what the size and shape of the finished pasta will be. When steel pins are placed in the holes of the die, the extruded tubular dough becomes a macaroni shape. If the pin has a notch on one side, the dough passes through that side faster and produces a slightly curved product. A variable-speed revolving knife cuts the dough from the face of the die to the desired length of the particular product.

Drying is a critical part of the manufacture of pasta. Pasta products are automatically conveyed into drying units, through which they move continuously during the drying process. Long items like spaghetti and vermicelli are hung on aluminum rods for their trip through the dryer. Short ones like elbow macaroni and special shapes are spread on aluminum slatted belts and drop from level to level as they are reduced in moisture.

Egg noodles, mixed in much the same way as macaroni and spaghetti but with the addition of a minimum of 5.5 percent egg solids (fresh, powdered or frozen) as required by law, are extruded through steel dies to form the width and thickness desired, and the revolving knife cuts the noodles from the face of the die to the predetermined length. Drying follows a procedure similar to that for other short forms of pastas.

For the most part, packaging of the finished macaroni products is accomplished by machine. Contents are weighed automatically and check-weighed either automatically or by the machine operator. Lasagne, twisted vermicelli and a few other special products still require hand packing.

Frozen Egg Noodles are flattened between rollers to form a thin, continuous sheet of dough, which is then automatically cut to the desired width and length. The pieces are then weighed and placed in the package and blast-frozen. After freezing, the product is stored at a temperature below zero degrees Fahrenheit. This temperature is maintained during shipment of the product to the supermarket in specially equipped freezer trucks.

THE NUTRITIVE VALUE OF PASTA

Pasta products, which form a part of the bread and cereal group, are a feature of the United States Department of Agriculture's Daily Food Guide. Four servings or more a day are recommended from this group, which also includes bread, cereal and other products made with enriched or whole-grain flour. Pasta, a natural food, contributes significantly in many ways to good health and fitness.

Pasta products are valuable sources of protein. They have a good distribution of six of the eight essential amino acids necessary for optimum health and growth. The other two amino acids are present in low amounts, but are easily supplemented by animal protein. Pasta products are usually served with meat, poultry, fish, seafood, cheese or eggs. These complement and round out the protein value of the pasta. The following figures compare the protein value (after cooking) of pasta products with other basic foods served alone and in traditional recipes.

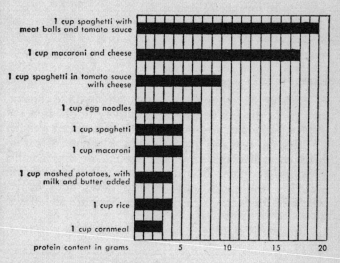

Source for chart facts: United States Department of Agriculture Home & Garden Bulletin No. 72, revised January, 1971.

An analysis of pasta products demonstrates the following:

Protein

	Protein Content
Macaroni and Spaghetti	12.5% to 13%
Egg Noodles	13% to 13.5%

Food Nutrients

All Skinner pasta products are enriched according to U. S. government standards. Four ounces (uncooked weight) of pasta provide the following proportions of the U. S. Recommended Daily Allowance for these essential food substances:

	Percentage of U.S. RDA
Protein	25%
Thiamine (Vitamin B_1)	70%
Riboflavin (Vitamin B_2)	30%
Niacin	40%
Calcium	2%
Iron	20%

Carbohydrates

Pasta products supply, through carbohydrate content, energy for growth and vigorous activity of children and stamina for adults. A 4-ounce serving (uncooked weight) of macaroni contains approximately 82 grams of carbohydrates, while the same size serving of egg noodles provides 80 grams of carbohydrates. For you weight watchers, the approximate caloric values of 4 ounces macaroni product weighed *after* cooking are as follows:

Product Weighing 4 Ounces After Cooking	Calories
Macaroni	155
Spaghetti	147
Egg Noodles	133

NOTE: 4 ounces of *uncooked* macaroni or spaghetti contain about 410 calories, 4 ounces of egg noodles *uncooked* contain about 430 calories. However, when pasta products are cooked, they absorb water, thereby increasing in weight. Therefore, 4 ounces of dry macaroni, after it is cooked, weigh several additional ounces. That is why 4 ounces of cooked macaroni have significantly fewer calories than the pasta in its dry state. Generally, the longer you cook pasta, the more water it absorbs (water has no calories) and therefore exact caloric content will vary upon the method and time of cooking.

Sodium

Pasta is a low sodium food, and can be enjoyed even on sodium-restricted diets. Analysis of cooked products shows average sodium content as follows:

	Milligrams per 100 Grams
Macaroni and Spaghetti	1.0 to 2.0
Egg Noodles	2.0 to 4.0

Fat

In view of doctors' concern over body cholesterol levels, it is fortunate that pasta products are considered low-fat foods. This is the average fat content:

	Percentage of Fat
Macaroni and Spaghetti	1.7
Egg Noodles	4.4

Digestibility

Pasta products are digested at a moderate rate and thereby provide not only energy, but satiety, preventing the return of hunger too soon after a meal. Thus they are suitable for the normal diet from early childhood on. The high digestibility of pasta is shown by these figures:

Nutrient	*Coefficient of Digestibility*
Carbohydrates	98%
Protein	85%
Fat	90%

SKINNER PACKAGE SIZE
METRIC EQUIVALENTS

8 ounces	227 grams
12 ounces	340 grams
16 ounces	454 grams
24 ounces	680 grams
2 pounds	907 grams
3 pounds	1.361 kilograms

METRIC CONVERSION TABLE*

Approximate conversions TO metric measures

When you know	*Multiply by*	*To find*
Weight		
ounces (oz.)	28.35	grams (g.)
pounds (lb.)	0.45	kilograms (kg.)
Volume		
teaspoons (tsp.)	5	milliliters (ml.)
tablespoons (Tbsp.)	15	milliliters (ml.)
fluid ounces (fl. oz.)	30	milliliters (ml.)
cups (c.)	0.24	liters (l.)
pints (pt.)	0.47	liters (l.)
quarts (qt.)	0.95	liters (l.)
gallons (gal.)	3.8	liters (l.)

Approximate conversions FROM metric measures

When you know	*Multiply by*	*To find*
Weight		
grams (g.)	0.035	ounces (oz.)
kilograms (kg.)	2.2	pounds (lb.)
Volume		
milliliters (ml.)	0.03	fluid ounces (fl. oz.)
liters (l.)	2.1	pints (pt.)
liters (l.)	1.06	quarts (qt.)
liters (l.)	0.26	gallons (gal.)

* Extracted from the Metric Conversion Card (revised August, 1975) published by the National Bureau of Standards, United States Department of Commerce.

INDEX

Al dente, definition, 196
All American Macaroni Casserole, 18
All Seasons Macaroni Salad, 88
Amandine, Noodles, 21
Anchovy Sauce, 75
Apple and Noodle Dessert, 106
Apple-Raisin Stuffing for Poultry, 51
Applesauce, Pork Chops with Apple-Spice Noodles, 39
As You Like It Spaghetti and Meat Balls, 14
Avocado, Guacamole, 80

Bami, 101
Barbecue Sauce, 174
Bavarian Creamed Egg Noodles, 140
Beef, Beef Dishes
  Burgers and Egg Noodles, Festive, 152
  Casserole, Hearty, Sam's, 32
  Chef's Casserole, 35
  Chili Mostaccioli, 35
  Curry with Noodles, 27
  Egg Noodles with Madcap Sauce, 160
  Flank Steak, Stuffed, 168
  Hamburgers, Holiday, 173
  Hungarian Goulash with Egg Noodles, 27
  Köttbullar and Egg Noodles, 15
  Lasagne, Classic, 95
  Lasagne, Easy, 29
  Lasagne à la Muriel, 16
  Lasagne, Quick, 126
  Lasagne Rolls with Meat Sauce, 96
  Lasagne-Style Noodle Casserole, 136
  Lasagne, Teenager's, 126
  Lasagnettes, 37
  Macaroni Casserole, All American, 18
  Macaroni and Cheese, Meaty, 168
  Macaroni with Chili Beef Sauce, 34
  Macaroni Meat Loaf, 29
  Macaroni Oriental, 104
  Macaroni Oriental (low-calorie), 149
  Macaroni Pastitsio, 94

  (and) Macaroni Salad, Dieters', 157
  Meat Ball Soup with Rings, 120
  Meat Ball Stroganoff, Quick, 134
  Meat Balls, Hungarian, with Noodles, 148
  Meat Balls and Spaghetti, Barbecued, 36
  Meat-Mushroom Sauce, 74
  Minute Steak with Herb Spaghetti, 153
  Mostaccioli Pie, 28
  Mostaccioli with Rich Tomato Beef Sauce, 37
  -Noodle Curry, 154
  Noodle Skillet Scramble, 165
  Party Macaroni Chili, 17
  Pot Roast, Old-Fashioned, 25
  Ragù Bolognese, 73
  Rigatoni, Baked Stuffed, 17
  Rigatoni with Onion Sauce, 123
  Roll, Stuffed, with Saffron Noodles, 99
  Sauerbraten and Ripplets, 26
  Seven-Way Sauce, 73
  Short Ribs, Italian-Style, 135
  Short Ribs and Macaroni, 28
  Skillet Supper, 112
  Sour Cream Noodle Bake, 130
  Spaghetti Americana "2000," 125
  Spaghetti Bolognese, 92
  Spaghetti with Extender Meat Sauce, 167
  Spaghetti and Meat Balls, 180
  Spaghetti and Meat Balls, As You Like It, 14
  Spaghetti with Meat Sauce, 33
  Spaghetti and Meat Sauce, Time-Saver, 109
  Spaghetti Milanese, 147
  Spaghetti Paisano for Company, 14
  Spaghetti Peppers, Barbecued, 173
  Spaghetti, Savory, 127
  Spaghetti with Swedish Meat Balls, 34
  Spaghetti with Tomato-Meat Sauce, 180
  Stroganoff Delight, 135

Beef, Beef Dishes (*Continued*)
Stroganoff with Noodles, 179
Tabasco Tomato Sauce, 71
Vermicelli with Herb Meat Sauce, 33
Belgium Macaroni Salad, 22
Bit-of-Turkey Casserole, 50
Broccoli, Ham, Macaroni, Casserole of, 182
Brussels Sprouts, Belgium Macaroni Salad, 22
Brussels Sprouts, Sunday Supper Ring, 65
Buffet Macaroni Salad, California, 24
Buffet Noodle Chicken Casserole, 19
Burgers, Hamburgers, *see* Beef
By-the-Seaside Salad, 84

California Macaroni Buffet Salad, 24
Capri Spaghetti Dinner, 103
Casey's Spaghetti with Cauliflower, 81
Cauliflower with Spaghetti, Casey's, 81
Cheddar, *see* Cheese
Cheese, Cheese Dishes
Cheddar Noodle Casserole, 61
Cheddar Cheese Sauce, 103
Colossus Almondine, 23
Eggs Goldenrod, 111
Filling (ricotta), 97
Lasagne, Classic, 95
Lasagne, Creamy, 97
Lasagne à la Muriel, 16
Lasagne, Quick, 126
Lasagne-Style Noodle Casserole, 136
and Macaroni, 145
and Macaroni Bake, Easy, 183
and Macaroni, Marvelous, with variations, 62
and Macaroni, Meaty, 168
and Macaroni Salad, 163
Macaroni Casserole, All American, 18
Macaroni Garden Salad, 143
Macaroni Salad, Belgium, 22
Macaroni Spinach Tortine, 82
Macaroni-Tomato au Gratin, 169
Manicotti, 58
Manicotti, Baked Stuffed, 30
Mostaccioli Casserole, 61
Noodle Ring, 60
Noodles Alfredo, 58

Ripplets with Three Cheeses, 59
Shrimp Supper, Cheesy, 112
Spanish Loaf, 64
Sunday Supper Ring, 65
Supremo, 62
Tuna Cheese Sauce, 72
Tuna Loaf, Cheesy, 185
Turkey-Cheese Meltaway Casserole, 50
Vermicelli Alfredo, 21
Vermicelli Parmesan, 63
Chef's Casserole, 35
Chicken, Chicken Dishes
Breasts with Creamy Noodles, 56
Cacciatori, Guest, 20
Cacciatore with Spaghetti, 159
Casserole, Four-Star, 184
Down-South Stew, 52
Fricassee with Noodles, Grandma's, 138
Fricasseed, with Spaghetti, 51
Kalakaua, 55
Macaroni Salad, 152
Marengo with Noodles, 54
Noodle Buffet Casserole, 19
and Noodles en Bianco, 150
and Noodles, Chinese-Style, 139
'n' Noodles, Old-Fashioned, 138
and Noodles in Wine Sauce, 101
Paprika, 53
in the Pot, Japanese, 102
-Ripplet Casserole, 53
Salad, Goddess, 131
Shell-Chicken Salad, 87
Spaghetti with Rich Sauce, 54
Spaghetti Royale, 55
and Spaghetti Skillet, 56
Stewed, with Dumplings, 123
Tetrazzini, 52
Vegetable Casserole, 137
Chicken Livers
Chicken-Lickin', 115
and Noodles, 154
Spaghetti with Chicken-Liver Sauce, 164
Chiletti and Franks, 166
Chili Mostaccioli, 35
Chili Spaghetti, 110
Chinese Lobster Macaroni, 129
Chinese-Style Chicken and Noodles, 139
Clams, Clam Dishes

Rigatoni Casserole, Creamy, 66
Seafarer's Pasta, 66
Seashore Slimmer, 156
Spaghetti with Clam Sauce, Family Favorite, 19
Colossus Almondine 23
Company Seafaring Noodles, 114
Confection, Noodle, 107
Crab, Crab Meat, *see also* Seafood
Macaroni Spring Salad, 155
Salad, Savory, 186
Spaghetti with Crab Sauce, 128
Cream Sauce, 31
Cream Sauce, Rich, 97
Creole Spaghetti Bake, 48
Curry, Curried
Beef-Noodle, 154
Beef, with Noodles, 27
Lamb, with Noodles, 47
Onion Sauce, 40
Pork with Spaghetti, 38
Shrimp, with Spaghetti, 185
Macaroni-Shrimp, 68
Turkey with Noodles, 144

Decorating with Pasta
beaded screen, 193
brooch, 193
cementing, 189
Christmas bell, 192
Christmas garlands, 192
Christmas stars, 192
Christmas tree ornaments, 191
Christmas wreath, 192
earrings, 193
Easter eggs, 192
flower pot covers, 194
jewel box, 193
macaroni jewelry, 192, 193
name pins, 193
pencil holder, 193
picture frame, 194
spray-painting, 190, 191
Deviled Eggs, 172
Deviled Macaroni Salad, 172
Deviled Spaghetti, 162
Dieters' Macaroni Beef Salad, 157
Dilled Shell Salad, 89
Dipsy Noodles, 79
Divine Turkey Medley, 49
Down East Chowder, 120
Down-South Stew, 52
Dumplings

Chicken, Stewed, with Dumplings, 123
with Prosciutto, 100
Salmon Dumpling Casserole, 67
Durum wheat, 195, 205

East Coast Rigatoni Casserole, 43
Egg Noodles, *see* Noodles
Eggplant Noodle Casserole, 19
Eggs, Egg Dishes
Bavarian Creamed Egg Noodles, 140
Deviled, 172
Deviled Macaroni Salad, 172
Goldenrod, 111
(and) Ham and Rigatoni Salad, 88
and Macaroni Bake, Creamy, 63
Macaroni Spring Salad, 155
Macaroni Superb à la Holstein, 128
'n' Noodle Salad, 161

Fall Macaroni Salad, 87
Family Favorite Spaghetti with Clam Sauce, 19
Fideo Laredo, 121
Filling, Cheese, 97
Fish, Fish Dishes, *see also* names of fish
Down East Chowder, 120
Macaroni Salad, Piquant, 155
Florentine Tuna Noodle Casserole, 161
Flounder, Roll-ups with Noodles, 65
Flour, 196
Four-Star Chicken Casserole, 184
Frankfurters, Frankfurter Dishes
Chiletti and Franks, 166
Gaucho Skillet Supper, 166
and Noodle Casserole, 169
Noodles with Kraut Frankfurter Sauce, 44
Picnic Spaghetti, 172
Sauce, "Red Hot," 74
Spaghetti with Chili-Frankfurter Sauce, 156
Spaghetti with "Red Hot" Sauce, 164
Fritters, Noodle, 170

Fruit Dishes
California Macaroni Buffet Salad, 24
Fruit Macaroni Salad, 90

Garden Fresh Salad, 133
Gaucho Skillet Supper, 166
German Macaroni Salad, Hot, 187
Goddess Chicken Salad, 131
Golden Gate Shrimp Bake, 140
Grandma's Chicken Fricassee with Noodles, 138
Greek-Style Stew with Macaroni, 102
Guacamole, 80
Guest Chicken Cacciatore, 20

Ham, Ham Dishes
Balls with Cranberry Sauce, 41
Casserole, 43
Deviled Spaghetti, 162
Dumplings with Prosciutto, 100
(and) Egg and Rigatoni Salad, 88
Fiesta, 122
(and) Macaroni and Broccoli, Casserole of, 182
Macaroni Milanese, 181
Macaroni Supper Salad Platter, 90
and Noodle Casserole, 151
Parma Noodles, 106
Ripplet Noodles Alla Milano, 106
-a-Roni, 160
Seashell Party Salad, 21
Tetrazzini, 42
Hamburgers, Burgers, *see* Beef
Hawaiian Pork Chops and Macaroni, 40
Hawaiian Shrimps and Macaroni, 104
Herb Meat Sauce, 33
Herb Spaghetti with Minute Steak, 153
Holiday Hamburgers, 173
Holiday Noodles and Hamburgers, 173
Hungarian Goulash with Egg Noodles, 27
Hungarian Meat Balls with Noodles, 148
Hurry-up Macaroni Tuna Casserole, 110

Italian Mostaccioli, 183
Italian Rigatoni Sauce, 98
Italian Spaghetti, Meatless, 181
Italian-Style Short Ribs, 135
Italian-Style Tomato Sauce, 72

Japanese Chicken in the Pot, 102
Jefferson House Speckled Noodles, 129

Köttbullar and Egg Noodles, 15

Lamb, Lamb Dishes
Curry with Noodles, 47
Macaroni with Greek-Style Stew, 102
Lasagne
Caesar Salad, 132
Classic, 95
Creamy, 97
Easy, 29
à la Muriel, 16
Quick, 126
Rolls with Meat Sauce, 96
-Style Noodle Casserole, 136
Teenager's, 126
Lasagnettes, 37
Lobster, Lobster Dishes, *see also* Seafood
By-the-Seaside Salad, 84
Macaroni, Chinese, 129
and Rigatoni, 105
Low-Calorie Recipes
Beef-Noodle Curry, 154
Chicken and Noodles en Bianco, 150
Curried Turkey with Noodles, 144
Festive Egg Noodles and Burgers, 152
Herb Spaghetti with Minute Steak, 153
Hungarian Meat Balls with Noodles, 148
Macaroni Beef Salad, Dieters', 157
Macaroni and Cheese, 145
Macaroni Chicken Salad, 152
Macaroni Garden Salad, 143
Macaroni Oriental, 149
Macaroni Salad Delight, 157
Macaroni Salad, Piquant, 155
Macaroni Salmon Salad, 148
Macaroni Spring Salad, 155
Noodle and Ham Casserole, 151
Noodles and Chicken Livers, 154

Seashore Slimmer, 156
Spaghetti with Chili-Frankfurter Sauce, 156
Spaghetti Milanese, 147
Spaghetti with Tuna Sauce,
145
Veal Cutlet-Macaroni Dinner,
146
White Sauce, A Basic, 162
Luncheon Meat Dishes
Macaroni Luncheon Bake, 47
Macaroni Salad, Fall, 87
Macaroni Salad, Picnic, 88
Noodle Pudding, Main Dish,
163
Spaghetti Entrée, Speedy, 114

Macaroni, definition, 196
Macaroni Elbows
All Seasons Salad, 88
Beef Salad, Dieters', 157
Bit-of-Turkey Casserole, 50
Brown Buttered, 122
Buffet Salad, California, 24
Casserole, All American, 18
Casserole Italiano, 110
and Cheese, 145
and Cheese, Marvelous, with
Variations, 62
and Cheese, Meaty, 168
and Cheese Salad, 163
Chicken Casserole, Four-Star,
184
Chicken Kalakaua, 55
Chicken Salad, 152
with Chili Beef Sauce, 34
Chili, Party, 17
Chinese Lobster, 129
Crab Meat Salad, Savory, 186
Down East Chowder, 120
Down-South Stew, 52
and Egg Bake, Creamy, 63
Eggs Goldenrod, 111
Fall Salad, 87
Garden Salad, 143
with Greek-Style Stew, 102
Gumbo, 117
(and) Ham and Broccoli, Casserole of, 182
Ham-a-Roni, 160
Loaf, 184
Luncheon Bake, 47
Meat Loaf, 29
Metro Minestrone, 118
Milanese, 181
Oriental, 104
Oriental (low-calorie), 149

Pastitsio, 94
Picnic Salad, 88
Rancho Salad, 89
Salad, Belgium, 22
Salad Delight, 157
Salad, Deviled, 172
Salad, German, Hot, 187
Salad, Norwegian, 89
Salad, Piquant, 155
Salad, Zingy, 22
Salmon Salad, 148
Sal-Mac Casserole, 113
Sausage Bake, 182
and Short Ribs, 28
-Shrimp Curry, 68
Shrimp Mousse, 86
Shrimp Salad, Best-Ever, 85
and Shrimps, Hawaiian, 104
Soup, Mushroom, 119
Spanish Loaf, 64
Spinach Tortine, 82
Spring Salad, 155
Superb à la Holstein, 128
Supremo, 62
Supper Salad Platter, 90
-Tomato au Gratin, 169
Tuna Casserole, Hurry-up, 110
and Tuna Garden Salad, 85
Tuna Loaf, Cheesy, 185
Tuna Supper Salad, 86
Turkey-Cheese Meltaway Casserole, 50
(and) Veal Cutlet Dinner,
146
Veal Scallops, Stuffed, Parmesan, 100
Zuppa Pasta Fagiola, 116
Macaroni Rings
Garden Fresh Salad, 133
Macaroni, Salad Mac
Fruit Salad, 90
Tomato Surprise, 187
Macaroni Shells
Beef Skillet Supper, 112
By-the-Seaside Salad, 84
and Cheese Bake, Easy, 183
Chicken Salad, Goddess, 131
Dilled Salad, 89
and Pork Chops, Hawaiian, 40
and Salmon, au Gratin, 186
Salmon Shell Salad, 86
Sam's Hearty Beef Casserole,
32
Seacoast Salad, 131
Seashell Appetizers, 80
Seashell Party Salad, 21
Shell-Chicken Salad, 87
with Shrimps, 111

Macaroni Shells (*Continued*)
Veal Casserole, 45
Macaroni Twirls, Gaucho Skillet
Supper, 166
Manicotti
Baked Stuffed, 30
Cheese, 58
Magnifico, 31
Meat, *see* Beef, Frankfurters,
Ham, Lamb, Luncheon
Meat, Meat Balls, Pork,
Sausage, Veal
Meat Balls
in Cream Sauce, 32
Hungarian, and Noodles, 148
Köttbullar and Egg Noodles,
15
Soup with Rings, 120
and Spaghetti, 180
and Spaghetti, Barbecued, 36
and Spaghetti, Quick, 113
Stroganoff, Quick, 134
Swedish, with Spaghetti, 34
Sweet and Sour, 38
Menus, Low-Calorie
Burger Bash, 151
Chicken Dinner, 150
Gourmet Meat Ball Dinner,
148
Hurry Curry, 144
Macaroni Cheese Supper, 144
Macaroni Patio Special, 147
Mandarin Mini-Dinner, 149
Milanese Spaghetti Dinner,
147
Savory Steak Dinner, 153
Slim-Down Noodle Dinner,
151
Summer Salad Special, 143
Trim Line Macaroni Meal,
152
Veal Cutlet Dinner, 146
Waist Watcher's Spaghetti
Supper, 145
Metric Table, 210
Metro Minestrone, 118
Minestrone, Noodle, 118
Mostaccioli
Beef Pie, 28
Cheese Casserole, 61
Chili, 35
Italian, 183
with Rich Tomato Beef Sauce,
37
Mousse, Shrimp Macaroni, 86
Mushroom
Gravy, Brown, 99
Macaroni Soup, 119

Meat-Mushroom Sauce, 74
Spaghettini, 64

Noodles, Egg Noodles, *see also*
Ripplets
Alfredo, 58
Amandine, 21
and Apple Dessert, 106
Apple-Raisin Stuffing for Poultry, 51
Apple-Spice, with Pork Chops,
39
with Beef Curry, 27
Beef-Noodle Curry, 154
with Beef Stroganoff, 179
Budapest, 59
and Burgers, Festive, 152
Cheddar Casserole, 61
Cheese Ring, 60
Chef's Casserole, 35
and Chicken en Bianco, 150
Chicken Casserole, Buffet, 19
and Chicken Livers, 154
with Chicken Marengo, 54
Chicken Paprika, 53
Chicken in the Pot, Japanese,
102
and Chicken in Wine Sauce,
101
Confection, 107
with Creamed Tuna, 69
Creamy, with Chicken Breasts,
56
with Curried Turkey, 144
definition, 196
Dipsy, 79
Egg Drop Soup, 119
Egg 'n' Noodle Salad, 161
Eggplant Casserole, 19
Flank Steak, Stuffed, 168
with Flounder Roll-ups, 65
and Frankfurter Casserole, 169
Fritters, 170
Ham Balls with Cranberry
Sauce, 41
and Ham Casserole, 151
Ham Fiesta, 122
and Hamburgers, Holiday, 173
how they are made, 196
with Hungarian Goulash, 27
with Hungarian Meat Balls,
148
and Köttbullar, 15
with Kraut-Frankfurter Sauce,
44
with Lamb Curry, 47
Lasagnettes, 37
with Madcap Sauce, 160

Minestrone, 118
Natasha, 170
(with) Old-Fashioned Pot Roast, 25
Onion Pie, 83
Parma, 106
Party Pancakes, 78
Pork Dinner, Oriental, 39
Pudding, Creamy, 107
Pudding, Main Dish, 163
Romanoff, 105
Saffron, with Stuffed Beef Roll, 99
-Salmon Scallop, 67
Seafaring, Company, 114
Skillet Scramble, 165
Soufflé of Egg Noodles, 167
Sour Cream Bake, 130
Speckled, Jefferson House, 129
Speedy Spanish Noodles, 122
and Squash Casserole, 130
Sunday Supper Ring, 65
Sweet and Sour Meat Balls, 38
Tuna Casserole, Florentine, 161
Tuna Hot Dish, 162
Turkey Medley, Divine, 49
with Veal Birds, 45

Noodles, Frozen
Beef Stroganoff Delight, 135
and Chicken, Chinese-Style, 139
Chicken 'n' Noodles, Old-Fashioned, 138
Chicken Vegetable Casserole, 137
Creamed, Bavarian, 140
with Grandma's Chicken Fricasee, 138
Lasagne-Style Casserole, 136
Meat Ball Stroganoff, Quick, 134
with Pork Tenderloin, 137
Short Ribs, Italian-Style, 135
Shrimp Bake, Golden Gate, 140
Skillet Tuna, 139
Norwegian Macaroni Salad, 89

Onion, Curry Onion Sauce, 40
Onion, Noodle Pie, 83
Oriental Macaroni, 104
Oriental Macaroni (low-calorie), 149
Oriental Pork Noodle Dinner, 39
Oysters, East Coast Rigatoni Casserole, 43

Pancakes, Noodle Party, 78
Parma Noodles, 106
Pasta
carbohydrate content, 208
definition, 195
digestibility, 209
drying, 206
economy value, 5
fat content, 209
food nutrients, 208
how it is made, 205
how much to buy, 6
how much to cook, 6
how to cook, 7
how to eat, 10
leftovers, 9
nutritive values, 207
packaging, 206
protein content, 208
shaping, 205-206
sizes, 197
sodium content, 209
Pastitsio, Macaroni, 94
Peppers, Spaghetti Peppers, Barbecued, 173
Picnic Macaroni Salad, 88
Picnic Spaghetti, 172
Pork, see also Ham, Sausage
Chops with Apple-Spice Noodles, 39
Chops and Macaroni, Hawaiian, 40
Curried, with Spaghetti, 38
Noodle Dinner, Oriental, 39
Spareribs, Barbecued, with Spaghetti, 41
Tenderloin with Noodles, 137
Poultry, see Chicken, Chicken Livers, Turkey
Pudding, Noodle, Creamy, 107
Pudding, Noodle, Main Dish, 163

Quantity Recipes
Beef Stroganoff with Noodles, 179
Chicken Casserole, Four-Star, 184
Crab Meat Salad, Savory, 186
directions for cooking large quantities of pasta, 177
German Macaroni Salad, Hot, 187
Ham, Macaroni and Broccoli, Casserole of, 182
Macaroni and Cheese Bake, Easy, 183

Quantity Recipes (*Continued*)
Macaroni Loaf, 184
Macaroni Milanese, 181
Macaroni Sausage Bake, 182
Macaroni Tomato Surprise, 187
Meatless Spaghetti, Italian, 181
Mostaccioli, Italian, 183
Salmon and Shell Macaroni au Gratin, 186
Shrimp Curry with Spaghetti, 185
Spaghetti and Meat Balls, 180
Spaghetti with Tomato-Meat Sauce, 180
Tuna Loaf, Cheesy, 185
Veal Birds Parmigiano, 178

Ragù Bolognese, 73
Rancho Macaroni Salad, 89
Ravioli, Inside-Out, 159
"Red Hot" Frank Sauce, 74
Rigatoni
Baked Stuffed, 17
Casserole Creamy, 66
Casserole, East Coast, 43
(and) Ham and Egg Salad, 88
and Lobster, 105
Milanese, 98
with Onion Sauce, 123
Sauce, Italian, 98
Rings, Meat Ball Soup with, 120
Ripplets, Ripplet Noodles
Chicken-Ripplet Casserole, 53
alla Milano, 106
Minestrone, 118
and Sauerbraten, 26
with Three Cheeses, 59

Saffron Noodles with Stuffed Beef Roll, 99
Salad Dressing, 132
Salads
By-the-Seaside, 84
Chicken, Goddess, 131
Crab Meat, Savory, 186
Egg 'n' Noodle, 161
Garden Fresh, 133
Ham, Egg and Rigatoni, 88
Lasagne Caesar, 132
Macaroni, All Seasons, 88
Macaroni Beef, Dieters', 157
Macaroni, Belgium, 22
Macaroni Buffet, California, 24

Macaroni and Cheese, 163
Macaroni Chicken, 152
Macaroni Delight, 157
Macaroni, Deviled, 172
Macaroni Fruit, 90
Macaroni, Fall, 87
Macaroni Garden, 143
Macaroni, German, Hot, 187
Macaroni, Norwegian, 89
Macaroni, Picnic, 88
Macaroni, Piquant, 155
Macaroni Salmon, 148
Macaroni Spring, 155
Macaroni Supper Platter, 90
Macaroni Tomato Surprise, 187
Macaroni and Tuna Garden, 85
Macaroni, Zingy, 22
Rancho Macaroni, 89
Salmon Shell, 86
Seacoast, 131
Seashell Party, 21
Shell-Chicken, 87
Shell, Dilled, 89
Shrimp, Best-Ever, 85
Shrimp Macaroni Mousse, 86
Tuna Supper, 86
Salmon, Salmon Dishes
Dumpling Casserole, 67
Macaroni Salad, 148
Noodle-Salmon Scallop, 67
Sal-Mac Casserole, 113
and Shell Macaroni au Gratin, 186
Shell Salad, 86
Spaghetti with Salmon Sauce, 165
Sam's Hearty Beef Casserole, 32
Sauces
Anchovy, 75
Barbecue, 174
Cheddar Cheese, 103
Cheese, 23
Cream, 31
Cream, Rich, 97
Curry Onion, 40
Frank(furter), "Red Hot," 74
Herb Meat, 33
Meat-Mushroom, 74
Mushroom Gravy, Brown, 99
Ragù Bolognese, 73
(for) Rigatoni, Italian, 98
Sausage, 75
Seafood, 72
Seven-Way, 73
Tomato, Basic, 71
Tomato Beef, Rich, 37

Tomato, Italian-Style, 72
Tomato, Tabasco, 71
Tuna Cheese, 72
Verde, 76
White, A Basic, 162
White, Rich, 94
White, Thin, 60
Sauerbraten and Ripplets, 26
Sausage, Sausage Dishes
  Casserole, Quick, 113
  East Coast Rigatoni Casserole, 43
  Lasagne, Creamy, 97
  Lasagne Rolls with Meat Sauce, 96
  Macaroni Bake, 182
  Macaroni Salad Delight, 157
  Minestrone, Noodle, 118
  Sauce, 75
  Spaghetti Paisano for Company, 14
Seacoast Salad, 131
Seafarer's Pasta, 66
Seafood, *see also* Clams, Crab, Lobster, Oysters, Shrimps
  Company Seafaring Noodles, 114
  Macaroni Gumbo, 117
  Sauce, 72
  Seacoast Salad, 131
Seashore Slimmer, 156
Semolina, 195
Seven-Way Sauce, 73
Shrimps, Shrimp Dishes, *see also* Seafood
  Bake, Golden Gate, 140
  Bami, 101
  Curry with Spaghetti, 185
  and Macaroni, Hawaiian, 104
  Macaroni Mousse, 86
  Macaroni-Shrimp Curry, 68
  Salad, Best-Ever, 85
  with Shell Macaroni, 111
  Supper, Cheesy, 112
Skillet Tuna Supreme, 139
Soufflé of Egg Noodles, 167
Soups
  Down East Chowder, 120
  Fideo Laredo, 121
  Macaroni Gumbo, 117
  Macaroni Mushroom, 119
  Meat Ball, with Rings, 120
  Metro Minestrone, 118
  Noodle Egg Drop, 119
  Noodle Minestrone, 118
  Vegetable, Hearty, 121
  Zuppa Pasta Fagiola, 116

Sour Cream
  Noodle Bake, 130
  Noodles Budapest, 59
  Noodles Natasha, 170
Spaghetti
  Americana "2000," 125
  with Barbecued Ribs, 41
  Bolognese, 92
  Capri Dinner, 103
  with Cauliflower, Casey's, 81
  Cheesy Shrimp Supper, 112
  with Chicken Cacciatore, 159
  Chicken-Lickin', 115
  with Chicken-Liver Sauce, 164
  and Chicken Skillet, 56
  Chicken Tetrazzini, 52
  Chiletti and Franks, 166
  Chili, 110
  with Chili-Frankfurter Sauce, 156
  with Clam Sauce, Family Favorite, 19
  with Crab Sauce, 128
  Creole Bake, 48
  with Curried Pork, 38
  definition, 196
  Deviled, 162
  Entrée, Speedy, 114
  with Extender Meat Sauce, 167
  with Fresh Tomato Sauce, 80
  with Fricasseed Chicken, 51
  Guest Chicken Cacciatore, 20
  Ham Tetrazzini, 42
  Herb, with Minute Steak, 153
  and Meat Balls, 180
  and Meat Balls, As You Like It, 14
  and Meat Balls, Barbecued, 36
  Meat Balls in Cream Sauce, 32
  and Meat Balls, Quick, 113
  Meatless Italian, 181
  with Meat Sauce, 33
  and Meat Sauce, Time-Saver, 109
  Milanese, 147
  Paisano for Company, 14
  Parmesan, 81
  Peppers, Barbecued, 173
  al Pesto, 13
  Picnic, 172
  with "Red Hot" Sauce, 164
  with Rich Sauce, 54
  Royale, 55
  with Salmon Sauce, 165
  Sausage Casserole, Quick, 113

Spaghetti (*Continued*)
  Savory, 127
  with Savory Veal Steak, 46
  Seafarer's Pasta, 66
  with Shrimp Curry, 185
  "Snack-a-Roni," 77
  Squares, 79
  with Swedish Meat Balls, 34
  with Tomato-Meat Sauce, 180
  with Tuna Sauce, 127, 145
  with Tuna Sauce (low-calorie), 145
  Tuna Tetrazzini, 68
  Veal Birds Parmigiano, 178
  with Veal and Peppers, 44
  with Vegetable Sauce, 93
  Vegetable Soup, Hearty, 121
Spaghettini, Mushroom, 64
Spanish Loaf, 64
Spanish Noodles, 122
Spinach Macaroni Tortine, 82
Stuffing, Apple-Raisin, for Poultry, 51
Sunday Supper Ring, 65
Swedish Meat Balls with Spaghetti, 34
Sweet and Sour Meat Balls, 38

Tabasco Tomato Sauce, 71
Teenager's Lasagne, 126
Tomato
  Beef Sauce, Rich, 37
  Macaroni Surprise, 187
  Sauce, Basic, 71
  Sauce, Italian-Style, 72
  Sauce, Tabasco, 71
Tuna, Tuna Dishes
  Capri Spaghetti Dinner, 103
  Cheese Sauce, 72
  Creamed, with Egg Noodles, 69
  Loaf, Cheesy, 185
  Macaroni Casserole, Hurry-up, 110
  and Macaroni Garden Salad, 85
  Noodle Casserole, Florentine, 161
  Noodle Hot Dish, 162
  Seafarer's Pasta, 66
  Skillet Tuna Supreme, 139

Spaghetti with Tuna Sauce, 127
Spaghetti with Tuna Sauce (low-calorie), 145
Supper Salad, 86
Tetrazzini, 68
Turkey
  Bit-of-Turkey Casserole, 50
  -Cheese Meltaway Casserole, 50
  Curried, with Noodles, 144
  Medley, Divine, 49

Veal, Veal Dishes
  Birds with Noodles, 45
  Birds Parmigiano, 178
  Casserole, 45
  Cutlet-Macaroni Dinner, 146
  and Peppers with Spaghetti, 44
  Scallops, Stuffed, Parmesan, 100
  Steak, Savory, with Spaghetti, 46
Vegetables, *see also* names of vegetables
  Chicken Vegetable Casserole, 137
  Metro Minestrone, 118
  Noodle Minestrone, 118
  Soup, Hearty, 121
  Spaghetti with Vegetable Sauce, 93
Verde Sauce, 76
Vermicelli
  Alfredo, 21
  Bami, 101
  Fideo Laredo, 121
  Ham Casserole, 43
  with Herb Meat Sauce, 33
  Parmesan, 63
  Seashore Slimmer, 156

White Sauce, A Basic, 162
White Sauce, Rich, 94
White Sauce, Thin, 60

Zucchini, Noodle and Squash Casserole, 130
Zuppa Pasta Fagiola, 116